Who Said I Wouldn't

Make It

Aileen Cunningham

Dedication

This book is dedicated to the memory of my beautiful mother, Dianna M. Reeves. Each day I strive to be all that you said I could be. I love you and long to see you again. Thanks for being my biggest cheerleader, and your legacy will live on.

Table of Contents

Introduction..5

Chapter One: The Story of Andrea/Can Life Really be This Good 6

Chapter Two: The Story of Sienna/The Change...24

Chapter Three: The Story of Tyrone/Just Pray the Mountain Will Move 40

Chapter Four: The Story of Jasmine/Could it Get Any Worse..54

Chapter Five: The Story of Noah/More Than a Conqueror...72

Chapter Six: The Story of Sharone/Looking For Love in All the Wrong Places 84

Chapter Seven: The Story of Carly/A Ray of Hope 96

Chapter Eight: The Story of Latisha/From Victim to Victorious...112

Chapter Nine: The Story of Stacy/You Can Make It 124

Chapter Ten: The Story of Tanya/Forgiveness = Freedom...146

Who Said I Wouldn't Make It

Introduction

Everyone has a story. Everyone has a past. Some people let the past rule them, holding on so tightly that it eventually destroys them; others see the past as a stepping stone to freedom. By the grace of an almighty God, I am part of the second group.

My desire, through this book, is to give hope to others who have struggled as I have. At the beginning of each chapter you will read a true story of a child that I encounter during my work as a child care provider. I want every person who reads my story to know that things can be different. There is a way out – Jesus Christ offers that hope. He has been my strength, protector, comforter and Savior – He wants to be that for you, too. Take the time to read this through and let Him move in your heart like He did in mine. My prayers are with you through your journey.

Chapter One

The Story of Andrea

Can Life Really be This Good

Andrea

Chapter 1 – Can Life Really be This Good

"For you created my inmost being; you knit me together in my mother's womb. I praise you because I am fearfully and wonderfully made . . . all the days ordained for me were written in your book before one of them came to be" (Psalm 139:13, 16).

Andrea grew up with her mama, but never knew her real father. Her mother seemed to have a new boyfriend every week and Andrea was used to strange men coming and going. When she was ten years old, her innocent world was shattered. Her mama's newest boyfriend stayed longer than the others. He ate dinner with them, went through their daily schedule with them, and looked like he could become her new daddy.

Andrea wanted a father and at first she was excited about this man. When he married her mother, Andrea finally thought she was part of a real family. Shortly after the wedding, their work schedules changed and he was home during the day while Andrea's mama was home at night. He was at the house every day when Andrea got back from school.

At first it started innocently enough. He gave her a hug when she got inside, then sat her down with a snack to talk about her day. The hugs became kisses on the cheek, then the lips and, to Andrea's horror, he started touching her in places she had never been touched. It kept getting worse, but he told Andrea it would kill her mother to know about them. She didn't want anything bad to happen to her mama and she didn't want to hurt her, so she stayed quiet. This continued for five years.

Finally, it became too much for Andrea. Her grades were dropping, she both hated and loved the man, and she couldn't handle lying to her mother anymore. She told a friend at school what was happening. The friend told the guidance counselor and the state did an investigation. Andrea's mama and the man denied it, but there was too much proof. He was arrested and Andrea was taken into state custody, and put into a home with an aunt.

Her aunt and therapist finally started convincing Andrea that it wasn't her fault, that the man had taken advantage of her and was wrong for what he'd done. They explained that any pleasure she felt wasn't because she was dirty, but because the human body was made to enjoy such things. They also told her that hating him and loving him at the same time was okay, but that eventually she needed to work toward forgiveness so she could move on. She didn't understand how she could hate and love someone at the same time, but the therapist said that if she talked to any other person who had been sexually abused, they would say the same thing.

It took Andrea a long time to work through all of that, but now she is a motivational speaker that goes from school to school talking to students about sexual abuse. She gets letters from girls and women around the nation who thought they were the only ones who had been through that, and found hope for the first time knowing they were not alone.

Chapter 1 – Can Life Really be This Good

"God saw my unformed body while I was still in my mother's womb" (Psalm 139). I shared that womb with two other baby girls. By the world's

standards, none of us should be alive today. We were born August 11, 1981, two and a half months before our due date. Adriana entered the world first, followed by Ayisha, then me. The doctor said chances were small that we would live long. Even if we survived, we would all be mentally retarded. Ayisha, the second born, was bleeding in the brain. To anyone looking on, it seemed hopeless. Yet, as tiny and fragile as we were, God had plans for us that no one else knew.

My father did not live with us, but unlike a lot of kids from single parent homes, we didn't miss his presence. Mama gave us the kind of life any child would want, and she was both mother and father to us. Before we were born, she made a promise to herself that she would give us the kind of life she never knew as a child. She wanted us to have everything she had missed out on while growing up. With all the strength she had, she was going to keep us happy and safe – that's what she told herself. The first step she had to take for that to happen was to leave my father. She lived with him, and she knew the way he treated her would be passed on to us. He was verbally and physically abusive, and she was not going to make her babies go through that.

Mama was a beautiful woman. She was successful with a college degree, steady job and personality that made everyone like her. Most people only have talents in a few areas, but she was talented in many ways. She worked with all kinds of people; those in communications, domestic violence situations, and abused kids. And she was creative. She could turn almost anything into an adventure.

Being a single parent to one child is a challenge, but triplets are on a whole different level. Mama worked constantly so she could give us what she thought we needed. From using cloth diapers and a diaper service to making our food at home instead of buying it at a store, she managed to do it all by herself. She worked long hours and sometimes hired nannies. At other times, she worked the night shift so she could have quality time with us during the day. Somehow she thrived at caring for all three of us through sickness, crying, feedings, diaper changes and playing. Her first priority was to be the perfect mother and prove to the world that against all odds, she was going to make it.

We were three very spoiled, but very happy, little girls. Our house had six bedrooms and we each had our own bedroom and bathroom, but our favorite was Mama's. It was a special treat for us to follow her into her bathroom, because it was so beautiful, decorated in pink and burgundy, with a whirlpool tub. We felt like princesses. The basement was set up as a recreation room where we could play and be as active as we wanted. It had a pool table, ping-pong table and lots of space to move around in.

Our daily routine was something we always looked forward to. Just as the sun started making its way up into the sky, I could hear Mama's footsteps coming up the stairs, the steps creaking every now and then. First she opened Adriana's door and said, "Good morning," in a sing-song voice. Then she moved to Ayisha's room, then mine. As soon as she had said good morning to each of us, she started singing to us from the hallway:

> *Good morning to you,*
> *Good morning to you,*
> *We're all in our places,*
> *With sun-shiny faces,*
> *This is the way we start our new day.*

By that time we were awake and singing the song with her, clapping our hands and climbing out of bed. She hugged each one of us when we went into the hallway, washed us up, and helped us get ready for the day. When breakfast was ready, she called out, "Little girls, come and eat!" She was a great cook, so we raced to the table. Breakfast was a special occasion every day. My favorite was her homemade blueberry muffins. She always made extras so we could take them to school. We were always excited about breakfast, knowing something delicious was waiting for us: cream of wheat, waffles, pancakes . . . While we ate, she sat and talked with us, then when we finished, she hugged each of us goodbye and sent us out to the school bus, waving as we pulled away.

At night, we had to memorize a Bible verse and say our prayers before we went to bed. Mama took this very seriously and even gave Ayisha a whipping one time when she was playing around instead of learning John 3:16. Adriana and I decided not to follow Ayisha's example, because we liked the way things were with Mama when we were obedient. We didn't like it when she had to discipline us, because it was so different from the happy, smiling mama we were used to. Parents sometimes tell their kids in the middle of discipline that it's harder for them than it is for the kids. I'm sure almost every child who hears that thinks, *You're not the one getting the bootie lash*

– how can this be hard on you? But in Mama's case, I believe it was painful for her. She wanted to have fun with us and pour love on us – she didn't like having to be hard on us for our disobedience any more than we liked receiving the discipline.

Mama usually drove us to church every Sunday and dropped us off, but sometimes she came in with us. She felt it was very important for us to attend and that we needed it. I wondered if it was because grown-ups had a choice about church and religion, and kids didn't. Either way, it wasn't an option for us – we were there faithfully because Mama made sure of it.

I didn't like being in church. I thought the people were fake and it seemed like a waste of my time. On the days that Mama stayed with us, I could see all the disapproving looks people around her gave us. She was a true worshipper – she wasn't quiet. She said, "AMEN," when she agreed with something the pastor said, raised her hands to heaven during worship, and put her whole heart into it. She was embarrassed and pulled back when some "leaders" of the church asked her to quiet down because it was disturbing the others. I believed the church was supposed to be a place people could go when they were hurting, but it seemed like they were the first ones to point out someone who was different and condemn them for it. I learned to believe that the church wasn't a safe place and that if I had a choice, I wouldn't be there.

Mama always let us sleep on the church pews. I was glad, because the sermons were boring. The pastor's voice stayed at one level and I didn't understand what he was saying. It wasn't until much later that the Bible the pastor was preaching from became really alive to me. In it were truths that I would cling to one day, and it would change and save my life forever. At the time, though, all I could see were plastic faces of people who didn't really seem to care about us underneath it all.

Since there were three of us and our mom, she called our mini-van the "Ladies 4." With all the places Mama took us and the activities we were in, that van was used a lot. Each of us had our own special activity, and Mama made a point not to miss any of our competitions or events. I was the dancer; Ayisha was in gymnastics; and Adriana was a swimmer.

I was the youngest and usually tried to do everything Ayisha did, which meant I wanted to go into gymnastics, too, but Mama encouraged me to choose something for myself that would make me unique. She introduced me to dancing and I ended up involved in ballet, tap, street jazz and modern jazz. It didn't take long for me to fall in love with it.

On weekends we each had our own appointments to practice and take lessons, but Mama was at every one of our competitions, shouting from the audience, "EXCELLENT!!" It was really embarrassing at the time, but I knew my mama was proud of me. I loved going to dance recitals and performing in front of crowds. My dance team and I often marched in parades and Mama was walking right along with me the whole way. This was an active part of my life for four or five years.

Mama kept things balanced and fair between us, but felt it was important for us to have our individual identities, too. She even dressed us alike, but we each had our own primary color. Mine was blue, Adriana's was red and, Ayisha's was yellow. We got a lot of attention because we were triplets. McDonald's even offered Mama a contract for us, but she didn't want to expose us to all the publicity and stress that could come with early fame.

Saturdays were always a treat for us. Mama loaded us into the van so we could have Steak N Shake day. It was almost as exciting for me as going out of town. I could imagine the taste of those big steak burgers and monster milkshakes before we even got there. I loved the French fries because they were so skinny, and I always called them "potaters." It was a great way to spend some of the weekend after five straight days of school. We got to hang out with Mama and just have a good time. We sat at the tables and talked and ate, laughing and loving life. Those were such great days for me that I still remember the smells and sounds as if they just happened. Every time I walk into a Steak N Shake, the memories of being there with my mama and sisters rush back to me.

Birthdays were a huge celebration for us. Since we were triplets, Mama went all out every year to have a "triple the fun" celebration. Our tenth birthday was the best. She invited all our friends from Girl Scouts over and each room was decorated with a different theme. One was set up for pillow fights, another for double dare, one for arts and crafts, and of course, the most important room was for Girl Talk. Mama turned the backyard into the slip and slide area and filled our four-foot tin pool so we could all swim. Our friends experienced a slumber party they would never forget.

It was pretty normal for Mama to have slumber parties with us. Most kids don't like having their parents around for things like that, but we loved it. Our house was the neighborhood hang-out spot. Mama was so much fun that all the other kids wanted to come over. Since the house was so big, we had lots of space to play between the basement, backyard and bedrooms. She even helped us set up a candy store in the garage called "Friendship Corner." All our friends came to buy candy from us. I never wondered what the other parents thought of her – I always called her the "Leave it to Beaver" mom, because it seemed she did everything right. I can imagine the other parents probably wished they had half the creativity and energy she had every day.

I think one of the struggles in single parent homes is that the parent is so busy trying to make ends meet that they forget sometimes their kids would rather miss out on a few dollars and have some affection instead. We didn't have that problem during the early years. Mama gave us lots of hugs and kisses, telling us every day how much she loved us. She wore her heart on her sleeve, and every ounce of affection she had poured out onto us all the time. We couldn't imagine what other kids were going through who didn't have a loving parent, who weren't safe and who didn't get everything their hearts desired. We had it all and even though we complained a lot, we loved it.

Some of our favorite times were setting up a tent in the backyard and "camping" out there. We spent full nights giggling and telling each other scary stories with the flashlight beams on our faces. One time Ayisha almost set the backyard on fire, because she tried building a bonfire like we had at Girl Scouts and other camps we went to. As we stayed in the backyard tent, we imagined we were really out camping somewhere else. There was always a stash of snacks, and we listened to the different bugs and night sounds that were all around us.

Those nights held us over between summers when we got to go to Christian family camp. The camp was a week-long event each summer sponsored by the church Mama took us to. An older white couple owned it and we looked forward to it every year. It was a week of swimming, volleyball, horses, arts and crafts, and great camp activities. We even learned Kum-Ba-Yah. I didn't know at the time that the song meant "Come By Here, Lord," but we felt like we were having a real camp experience when we learned it.

I'm not sure how much the adults looked forward to having us there, because we were always getting into trouble, but we had a good time. One year I was there with a half cast on my leg. I felt sorry for myself because I couldn't go swimming with the others, and Ayisha had just taught herself to swim in the deep end. Other than our little pool in the backyard, I'd never been swimming, so Ayisha decided she was going to help me cut the cast off. It was interesting figuring out the best way to do it, but between the two of us, we got it off and she taught me how to swim in the deep end for the first time. As soon as Mama saw us, we knew we were in trouble. She had that scary mama voice when she said, "WHAT HAVE YOU DONE?!?!" Even though we suffered for it later, I don't regret that we did it.

Mama took us on a lot of trips, including Disney World. The first time we went was when we were five years old. Her boyfriend at the time had us cramped into his car and we were so excited that every hour we asked if we were there yet. I know we must have been getting on the grown-ups nerves by the second or third hour, but they were patient with us. Mom was almost as excited as we were, because it was our first trip to Disney World – she was having as much fun watching us enjoy it as we were experiencing everything for the first time.

When we got into the theme park, I found myself surrounded by sounds and sights I had never experienced. There were bright colors all around, hundreds of people, Disney characters walking around getting their pictures taken with the kids, music blasting from the sound system, rides everywhere I looked . . . I was so excited I could hardly stand still. I couldn't figure out which place I wanted to go first, because there were so many to choose from. I could smell funnel cake and hamburgers as I saw eight-inch lollipops and cotton candy in kids' hands.

My sisters and I each got Mickey and Minnie stuff to wear, and we had the little hats with Mickey ears. Then we got our own cotton candy. We went on all the kiddie rides and got our pictures taken with the Disney characters. We were all smiles as we ran from place to place, chatting excitedly about where we were going to go next.

On one of the nights, Mama thought it would be fun to take us to a dinner theater that was showing the Three Little Pigs. Unfortunately, the big bad wolf scared us so bad that all three of us broke into terrified tears and had to leave early. I guess we were a little sheltered, but it was just too much for us to take. On the way home, we were more peaceful because we had tired ourselves out on our trip. Other similar vacations followed that one, and each had its own special place in my childish world.

To this day, I don't know how Mama did so much for us. In my eyes, she was the most perfect mom in the world and her endless enthusiasm, creativity and love seemed like they could never run out.

Chapter Two

The Story of Sienna

The Change

Sienna

Chapter 2 – The Change

"You are my hiding place; you will protect me from trouble and surround me with songs of deliverance" (Psalm 32:7).

Sienna was fifteen years old when she found out she was pregnant. She and her brothers and sisters had no set schedule, and were free to run around whenever and wherever they wanted. It was normal for them to get in fights with other kids in the neighborhood, but they stuck together and were proud of who they were. They thought their lives were great. They believed the fights they got in, and the bruises and scars they carried, were trophies.

It hit them hard when someone turned their mama in for neglect. Sienna was put into a foster home and had a miscarriage shortly after her placement. At that time she went into a children's home. She tried not to tell anyone about it, but eventually started trusting a few people. Their reactions were not what she expected. Their eyes filled with tears – for her. She couldn't remember anyone ever crying for her and it made her uncomfortable, but she still told her story.

When she finished telling it, those people pulled her into their arms and said, "That must have been so hard." They were Christian people and she expected to hear them say, "Well, that's what you get for doing things you shouldn't have been doing," or, "That's God's punishment for what you did."

She pulled away and asked, "Aren't you going to judge me?"

One of the women said, "Sienna, not one of us can come to you and say we've never messed up. Sometimes attitudes of pride and judgment are far worse than any act with the body. Every one of us is weak in some area. All of us have been places we had no business being in. What you've done makes you just as human as the rest of us."

She couldn't figure it out. She'd been watching these people for awhile and she knew something was different about them. Finally, she had to ask. They started telling her about their own lives and where they had been when God got a hold of them. She was amazed. They all could have been her. At that time, she knew she wanted to be where they were. She wanted to have what they had, so she asked Jesus to be her Savior.

Sienna went through a life change that no one could have imagined. She went from being hard and leading people in the wrong direction to being a natural leader that led people to the One who could give them real life. To this day she doesn't regret her decision to turn away from the things she knew before in order to become a child of God.

Chapter 2 – The Change

In a way, it was kind of a miracle that Mama was able to do such a great job with us, considering where she came from. Her years growing up were far from perfect. Her mother died when she was three years old and she was left with an alcoholic father who couldn't take care of his five children. He gave them up to state custody, and they were placed in different children's homes and foster families.

The fear my mother experienced of living day to day, not knowing if this was the day she would be suddenly picked up and taken somewhere else or if she could stay just a little longer. She and her siblings never knew what to expect in the foster homes. Some places were okay and the people took care of them, but others were a nightmare. In one place the foster dad abused Mama's brother by putting him in scalding bath water. In others, they were treated like criminals and forced to live in a military-like setting with very little freedom. Mama was moved more times than she can remember and had no control of it. One family would decide they no longer wanted foster children, another decided they wanted boys instead of girls, the state decided it was an unfit home . . . the reasons came in different shapes and forms, but they all resulted in one thing – Mama decided it was safer not to get attached to any of them. If she settled in, it would all be taken from her before she could blink.

In different circumstances, Mama might have been close to her family, but because they were separated and each had their own experiences to survive through, the decision not to get too close to anyone included each other. Besides, every time they were together was a reminder of all they had lost. Their mother was dead, their father didn't want them, and couldn't take care of them even if he did. People they stayed with didn't see them as their own children and they were passed around like objects instead of human beings.

Mama's last foster home was the best and she felt herself getting attached to them, believing they were actually going to keep her, and they probably would have, but both of the foster parents died and she had to move again. She had no chance to grow roots any one place, because she never knew how long she would be there.

One of the biggest struggles Mama faced as she grew up and entered her adult years, was the feeling that her father betrayed them and that it would have been better for them to stay together with him as a family, even if he did have problems. It took years for her to get over her anger, both because he gave them up and because he didn't take care of them the way a father should. He passed away when my sisters and I were thirteen, but thankfully before he was gone, Mama forgave him and reconciled their relationship.

I grew up hearing people talk about how the sins of the parents pass on to the children, and at the time I didn't know what that meant and honestly, I didn't care. Even if I had, I wouldn't have believed it could happen to us. All I could see was that I had an amazing mother, loved my sisters, and couldn't imagine life being any better. I had no idea what disappointing cruelty faced me.

When I was about six or seven, some major, terrible things happened in my mama's life, and the grief and guilt that came with them began to eat her up inside. The most important parts of her character began to dissolve, one piece at a time. She also still held tightly to the promise she made of being the perfect mother and the weight of it started becoming too much. Instead of trying to work through the guilt and grief of the things she went through as a child and choices she made as an adult, she went into a deep depression. Like most parents, I don't think she believed we noticed or understood the changes in her. Children are much more perceptive than their parents realize. And parents aren't as good at hiding things as they think they are.

She slept all the time and began drinking. She didn't want us to know it, so she hid her bottles in laundry hampers, underneath piles of clothing, or in the backs of cupboards, hidden by cleaning supplies. Our routine suddenly looked very different. I can't describe the shock of having to adjust from the vibrant, energetic, loving woman she was to the empty shell she was becoming. Until this point, our ritual after we got home from school was to sit at the table with Mama, eating a snack and talking about our day. When she started getting depressed, everything changed. She was still in bed by the time we got home, and I went into her room every day and said, "Mama, we're home. Are you going to get up today? Please, Mama, are you okay?" Most of the time, she didn't respond at all. It was like I was talking to a dead body that had once been my beloved hero. Other days I tried to stay out of her way, because I didn't know what would set her off. Sometimes her moods were okay, but at others, it seemed as if a misunderstood look would be enough to upset her.

I was so scared. I missed Mama the way she used to be so much and all I wanted was to help her feel better, but I didn't know how. At that time, my little girl carefree life took a cruel turn that forced me to feel grown-up stress. I knew something was seriously wrong, but as a child there was very little I could do about it. My understanding of things was so simple – so innocent. My heart was breaking as I watched Mama deteriorate, and it was completely out of my control.

By the time we were nine years old, the effort she

had put into us along with the continued guilt and depression caused a gradual breakdown. She was weak and worn out. The pressure she had put on herself to do everything perfectly was too much. She started hanging out with the wrong people and drinking more and more. Even as she preached anti-drug agenda to my sisters and I, I knew she smoked weed down in the basement and tried to cover it up. I lost respect for Mama as an example to follow, yet I loved her and wanted her to be okay. I was thrown back and forth between anger that she wasn't the woman she used to be and love for her. Both constantly raged war against each other inside of me. I wanted to protect her, because the torture of what life would be like without her was too much to think about.

Some of the most terrifying moments of my life were nights when my sisters and I stared out my bedroom window at crazy hours waiting for Mama to come home. It was well past our bedtime, but there was no way we could sleep as long as she was out there and we didn't know what was happening to her. From my bedroom we could see the driveway. We knew she was somewhere either drinking or getting high, or in her car after she was already drunk or high. Our hearts pounded as the cruelty of our imaginations sent pictures through our heads that no child should see. My imagination was my worst enemy, and the question that tortured me was, "What if . . . ?"

In those moments we did the only thing we could think of – we held hands and prayed that God would bring her home safe. As we waited, wanting her car to turn the corner, I felt stress and pain from a burden that no child should ever have to carry. I didn't know if this would be the night we became orphans or if Mama would show up at any moment, drunk but safe. I knew Mama had worked hard for us, but the responsibility forced on me of fearing for her life and wondering if she would come home, or if she had abandoned us, was an unfair match to her responsibility of having to raise us.

The tension between us did not ease up until we knew she was safely inside the house. We could hear her car as soon as she turned onto our street, and our grip on each other's hands tightened as we heard the loud music and saw her car speeding toward the house. I held my breath as she skidded into the driveway and parked in a crazy position because she was too drunk to notice. I watched while she fumbled with her keys, sometimes dropping them or having to go through several before finding the one to let her into the house. As soon as the door closed behind her, I was able to breathe and for a few hours, I felt peace again. It was okay with me that she didn't come upstairs to check on us, because at least under our roof she was safe and, for one more day, I still had a mother.

Since we spent so many late nights waiting up for Mama, staying awake in school was a struggle. On top of that, I was starting to get in trouble in my classes. In third grade alone I got suspended four times. I didn't like what was happening at home and I acted out at school because of it. I was determined that no one was going to see how scared I was all the time, so I hid behind the face of a bully. I made other kids afraid so they wouldn't see the real me. My biggest outlet was fighting.

One time I went to school and as usual, I hadn't done my homework the night before, so I tried to convince a girl in my class to let me cheat off her paper. I had a tutor, but I just didn't understand the work, so I cheated as much as I could. She was a good girl and didn't want any problems, but she was embarrassing me a little about not getting my work done. I threatened that as soon as the teacher let us take a bathroom break, I was going to beat her up in the bathroom. Since I had said it, I knew I had to follow through or else the other kids would know I wasn't as tough as I acted.

When we got into the bathroom, I shoved the girl and said, "What the *&@&* do you think you're doing talking to me like that?" The girl really didn't want to fight me, but I was already attacking her, so she had to fight back a little just to defend herself. I was stronger, so I dragged her into one of the stalls and tried to shove her head in the toilet. The other kids ran and got the teacher, and I ended up having to wait in the principal's office until I could call Mama and tell her what happened.

Another time I hit a boy on the head with a book because he wouldn't give me something I wanted, and he ended up having to get stitches. I was a bully. I disrespected my teachers and peers, even going so far as to break into my teacher's closet during recess to get to her M&M stash because she wouldn't give me any for completing my homework. I didn't care that I didn't deserve them because I hadn't done my homework – I just wanted the candy. I stole from other kids, cussed teachers out and basically did everything Mama had taught me not to. She had taught me to respect people; answer with "Yes, Ma'am," or "No, Sir." She never cussed around us, but I knew all the words and had creative ways of using them. Mama taught us to tell the truth, but I lied all the time.

At home I was becoming the same way. Not only had Mama spoiled us to the point that we were rotten through and through, but now she wasn't even the woman she had been and didn't have the energy to deal with us. We were angry and spoiled, and turned it on her. Any time she asked us to do something small around the house like clean up our rooms or wash the dishes, we mouthed back at her, making things harder on her than they already were.

Mama finally decided it would be better for me to go to a new school, separated from my sisters. I came home from school one day and she sat me down at the kitchen table. She said, "Baby, I love you, but some things need to change. I've tried everything, but nothing seems to be working. You're going to be moving through a big transition in your life, but I believe it's for the best. Until you can show me that your behavior has improved, you will be going to a different school than your sisters. I don't want to do this, but it's my last option."

I was in shock. I was terrified. I had never been separated from my sisters and always had them there to back me up if I needed it. Going to a new school left so many questions in my mind and so many frightening possibilities. I had no idea what to expect. What would the teachers be like? Would the kids see through me and realize I was just a scared girl? What would happen to me? The one sure answer was that I needed to get my act together, because the most terrible punishment Mama could have given me was separating me from my sisters.

She was hoping I would do better in a different environment. I didn't. I kept on getting in trouble. At the time I didn't understand or really care why I was acting up. I took everything our mama taught us and did for us for granted. I was still angry because my perfect home life wasn't so perfect anymore.

Mama was already struggling, but things got even harder when she crushed her pelvic bone at work and couldn't work full time anymore. Her depression got worse and made it more difficult to even pay the bills, let alone giving us extra things like she had before. I remember times that I would come home from school to a cold. I never knew what

Mama's moods would be like and I was constantly on edge trying to figure out what to do.

Chapter Three

The Story of Tyrone

Just Pray the Mountain Will Move

Tyrone

Chapter 3

Just Pray the Mountain Will Move

"May He send you help from the sanctuary, and strengthen you out of Zion" (Psalm 20:2).

Tyrone was as hard as a person can get. He could convince most of his peers to do whatever he wanted, including taking the blame for something he had done, even if it meant they went to juvenile detention for it.

People in Tyrone's life warned him that eventually it would catch up with him, but he just laughed and said, "No, it won't." For awhile it seemed as if he was right, but while he was out on the streets, fighting other gangs and dealing drugs, he thought he was living the high life. He believed no one could touch him – that he was invincible.

Tyrone made enemies pretty regularly, but he thought it was a game. He said it made life an adventure. One day he was on a porch with some of his friends when one of the men he had crossed came up to them and started shooting. He was trying to hit Tyrone, but anyone in the way went down, too. Tyrone's girlfriend was one of them. When the scene cleared, police had been called and the reports came out. Tyrone was paralyzed from the neck down because he'd been shot in the spine, his girlfriend was dead, and a couple of his other friends had permanent injuries. Suddenly, Tyrone's life wasn't looking so fun anymore.

He is now in a special facility for quadriplegics and has to have staff do everything for him. Things he took for granted, like eating and using the bathroom, are now humiliating parts of every day for him. Since he can't do much, he has plenty of time to think and suffer with the guilt of his past. All the people who suffered because of his decisions parade through his mind constantly – and he can't take any of it back.

Chapter 3

Just Pray the Mountain Will Move

My sisters and I started going to our dad's house for weekend visits. We liked going there because he gave us everything we wanted, while Mama couldn't. We disrespected her even more during that time, rubbing it in that Daddy was giving us so much and she wasn't. She started threatening to make us stay with him if we didn't get it together, and she knew we didn't really want that to happen. Each time she threatened, we decided to behave ourselves, but it only lasted for a little while.

By this time, I was back at school with my sisters, because the school I had been sent to only went through fifth grade. I loved being back with my sisters and, for a time, I tried to behave myself, but that fighting, angry spirit was still part of me and I didn't act the way I should have.

When we were twelve years old, it became too hard for our mama to manage us on her own. She resented Daddy for taking so little responsibility for us. He was living the life he wanted with no strings attached, and she wanted a taste of that. She wanted to be free. I didn't have any idea how much like a prisoner she felt and if I had known at the time, I would have felt like she didn't want us anymore – like we were a burden that she would gladly give up . . . a complete rejection.

One day in sixth grade, I started arguing with a girl who said Ayisha's boyfriend was really her boyfriend. Instead of focusing on the fact that the boy was really the one at fault, I got defensive of my sister and told the girl she needed to get used to the idea that he was Ayisha's boyfriend and not hers. At first she just cussed me out, but since I had a reputation to keep, I didn't back down. She punched me and while I fought back, I knew she was stronger than me, so she started getting the best of me. The bus driver stopped the bus, went all the way back to school, and told the principal we were fighting. One person held onto me as we walked back to the principal's office, but no one was holding onto her, so she took another shot, hitting me in the back of my head.

When I got home and Ayisha saw me, and I told her the whole story, she got some peroxide and medicine, and tried to clean me up. At first she was saying how sad it made her that someone did this to her sister, but the more she talked, the angrier she got. Finally, she decided she was going to pay the girl back for what she'd done to me. When I went to get my suspension letter from school the next day, Ayisha went with me and fought the same girl. She got suspended, too. Since spring break was close, Mama told us our punishment would be staying with our dad for spring break while Adriana stayed with her. Adriana usually didn't get involved in the messes Ayisha and I got into, and sometimes I know she felt left out, but she ended up with fewer regrets.

Ayisha and I stayed with our dad that week, but when it was over, Mama didn't come to get us. We were so mad at her that when she called to see if we were ready to come home yet, we said no. This went on for a few weeks. Daddy was still being nice to us and we were bitter that she would leave us like that. Shortly after Easter, she dropped Adriana off, too. She decided it was time to live her life and that our dad needed to take responsibility for us. Needless to say, he and our step-mama weren't happy.

Daddy had no idea how to be a real father. If my mama's years growing up were hard, his were just as bad. He was the youngest of three kids and while he had both parents, his family was full of alcoholics.

None of them showed affection. They thought if the kids were getting fed, clothed and sheltered, that was all the love they needed. My grandfather was blind and had other health problems due to his lifestyle; he died when Daddy was in his twenties or thirties. Since they had such a sad, almost non-existent relationship, my dad hardly ever said anything to us about our grandfather.

My grandmother was a twin and died when we were six years old. Daddy was close to her and talked about her a lot. Her twin sister took the place as his mother and our grandmother. After our grandmother died, our great aunt seemed to be the only woman Daddy listened to with any respect.

Unfortunately, his aunt died the same year that his brother died of heath problems and his sister died of stomach cancer. Daddy was so bitter, always talking about how he was the only one left in his family. In spite of this, he still failed to see that he was in the same destructive pattern that his family had been in – alcohol controlled him.

Our relationship with our father was similar to the one he had with his dad. We always thought of him as a holiday dad, because he brought gifts on special occasions, but that was about it. He had another son and daughter by two different women, but they didn't have much of a relationship with him either. They both called him by his first name. My half-sister actually thought he was her uncle for a long time.

Out of all of us, Daddy tried the hardest not to have a relationship with his son, but he had never been taught what a real father was like, so he did not know how to be one. Finally, he and my brother stopped speaking, leaving them both bitter and hurt. One time my brother said to me, "Ask your dad what I ever did to make him stop loving me." I couldn't forget the pain in his words. What Daddy didn't expect was that his son would also pass away before him, never knowing how much his father really loved him. My dad lived the life he wanted to and refused to allow anyone to tie him down. He was a fire chief and police officer, successful in his career, but failing miserably in his personal life.

Daddy thought that if the women in his house weren't cooking, cleaning or doing his laundry, they were a waste of space. He let everyone know he wasn't happy about it if he had to do something himself. We realized we were his burden, not his children. He never told us he loved us, and believed we should be grateful to him for feeding us and putting a shelter over our heads. We were being greedy if we expected more than that. I don't think he understood how to emotionally attach to anyone. In that environment it was no surprise that my sisters and I were on edge, so we started fighting all the time. Children watch the people around them and start to model their behavior.

Our way of communicating was to cuss, scream and get physical to prove our point. A typical day looked like this: Ayisha and Adriana started arguing about who used the curling iron last. After some yelling and screaming, Ayisha started threatening to throw the iron at Adriana and since Ayisha always found weapons to use whether it was a shoe or a hot curling iron, we knew she would use them. At this point, Ayisha usually took the first move into physical fighting, which ended up in a fistfight that I had to break up. The combination of who was fighting who changed around and I was involved in it just as much as the other two, but that was usually the type of situation that started fights.

We were almost as bad as Daddy with how we talked to each other. We called each other every foul name we could think of and ripped each other apart using every personal weapon we could. Yet when it came down to someone else messing with one of us, we protected each other as far as we had to go.

For the first few months that we lived with our father, we didn't see him much. He worked long hours, so our step-mom, Regina, took care of us. The first year was okay, but that was the honeymoon period. Regina gambled and our dad drank. They argued all the time. Daddy believed women were beneath him, so he didn't treat her right. She was home with us most of the time and didn't have much to look forward to where he was concerned.

During those months living with our dad, Mama was in the party scene, hanging out with drug users and becoming a completely different woman from the one we had known before. Often she ended up drunk and in situations she never meant to get into. People took advantage of her when she was intoxicated. She often woke up in strange places, next to a stranger, with no idea what happened.

After a few months, Daddy took her to court for custody, but because she didn't show up, he won. She was already a mess, but when she found out she had lost us, she became even more depressed, and her drinking and lifestyle got worse. She tried calling us, but Daddy wouldn't let us talk to her. Sometimes he cussed her out and hung up on her. Then he'd turn on us, say something mean about Mama, and when we told him not to talk about her that way, he cussed us out and told us how stupid we were to still love her after what she'd done to us.

Every time I heard the phone ring, I felt torn between excitement and fear. My heart started racing and felt like it would beat right out of me. I wanted to hear her voice, because it meant one more day that she was alive. I dreaded and half expected a phone call with some impersonal police officer telling us she was dead and there was no hope that we would ever be with her again. My mama; the woman who had carried me inside her for nine months. I felt everything that happened to her almost as if it happened to me. I felt responsibility for everything she did and everything that happened to her. I had no control over any of it, but I still felt it.

There were times Mama called and she wouldn't say anything, but we could hear street sounds in the background. I think she just wanted to hear our voices. We knew it was her, but she stayed silent. Daddy didn't know what our lives had been like with our mama before we were with him, so he didn't know just how much reason we had to love her even though things were rough. He kept trying to convince us that leaving us with him and not coming back proved that she didn't care about us, but inside we knew the truth and held onto it. We learned fast that the safest thing was not to talk about her around him.

Sometimes we asked Daddy to take us over to Mama's house to make sure she was okay. The only times he actually did this were if he'd had a really good day or wanted to get money from her, or help from her in some way. The car ride was about five minutes, but it always seemed so much longer. The same questions ran through my mind over and over. Would Mama still be alive? Would she be home? What would we find when we got there? The tension during the ride, and never knowing what to expect when we got there, was a huge strain.

There were times when we still lived with her that it seemed as if a dark presence was tormenting her. Sometimes she played gospel music full force, had all the lights turned off, and would beat things with a metal bat. It was terrifying for us – we had no idea what to do or think when she started doing that. Sometimes when Daddy took us there we could hear the music from outside, but she wouldn't answer the door. We saw her looking out at us from a window, but she didn't let us in. In those moments, I wanted to cry and scream at her to let us in. I felt abandoned and neglected. It made me wonder if what Daddy told us really was true. Maybe she didn't love us anymore. I wanted time to rewind to the way things had been, but I knew it wouldn't happen that way.

It was as if her past was chasing her, torturing her day after day. Instead of fighting it, she gave in, letting it destroy her. In spite of her fear, she didn't stay away from dangerous situations. Her lifestyle could have cost her life, but she was in so deep that she didn't seem to realize or care. She was lonely and hurting, and reached out to the wrong people. She craved love and acceptance, but never found them in the places she looked. In the end, she feared people almost as much as she feared herself.

One day it got so bad that while Mama was at a rundown apartment complex, she tried to come on to a man while she was intoxicated. He turned her down, but she was persistent, so he stabbed her in the neck. To this day she carries the scar from that. It was moments like those that I was sure we would lose her. Every day I waited, just knowing this would be the last day, constantly in a state of anxiety because at least while we lived with her, I knew when she came home at night. While we lived with Daddy, I didn't know anything. Her life could end in the daylight or by night.

Stress and fear were my closest companions. Even with all the things that had happened, I loved her and worried about her all the time. When Daddy wasn't around, my sisters and I tried to call her, not knowing if we would even be able to find her. She had lost so much: her kids, her self-dignity and her fight to keep us from going through what she had been through as a girl.

Chapter Four

The Story of Jasmine

Could it Get Any Worse

Jasmine

Chapter 4 – Could it Get Any Worse

"O Lord, my strength and my fortress, My refuge in the day of affiliation, The Gentiles shall come to you from the ends of the earth and say. Surely our fathers have inherited lies…" (Jeremiah 16:19).

Jasmine's parents died when she was two years old. Her godmother, Michelle, took her in and for a few years it was just the two of them. Jasmine loved her adoptive mama and everything seemed perfect. Then Michelle got married and everything changed.

David seemed okay at first, but as pressures at work started building up, he began drinking a lot. At first he would yell at them for small things or things he imagined they had done. Then it became more personal and he called them fat and lazy, anything that would hurt them.

The emotional beatings were bad enough, but it didn't stop there. After awhile David told Michelle she wasn't disciplining Jasmine enough and that she needed to let him take over. Michelle fought him on it, but by then he had beaten her spirit down so much that she was no match for him. First it was his belt, but then he started getting more creative. Unfortunately, he was careful about where he hit her and there were never marks in places that could be seen by anyone at school. She was afraid that if she told anyone about it, he would kill her or Michelle.

He started getting careless though. He lost all reasoning when he was beating her and Michelle was powerless to stop him. Finally in desperation, she sent in an anonymous hotline call from her office. After the investigation showed bruises on Jasmine's body, the case workers took Jasmine from the home and placed her in an emergency facility until something else could be found.

David was put in anger management classes and Michelle was told she could not have Jasmine back unless she was able to prove she could keep her safe. The only option Michelle believed she had was to leave David, put a restraining order against him, and try to start over.

Jasmine had learned to harden herself by this time, and it took awhile to convince her that Michelle had started a new life for them where she would be protected. When Jasmine was in high school, she started attending church with a friend from school. When she walked into that building, she felt something she had never felt before. It was as if something invisible was wrapping its arms around her, welcoming her home. It had been years since she felt so safe.

As the pastor explained who Jesus Christ is and what He did on the cross, Jasmine saw for the first time that she could belong to a whole family and that she really could be protected. On that day, she gave her life to Jesus and then went on to share everything she learned with Michelle, who then also believed in Him.

Jasmine is now a college student, studying business so she can open up centers for battered women and their children. She actively mentors kids in the state system who have gone through the same things she has. She wants them to know that they also can have hope.

Chapter 4 – Could it Get Any Worse

I was in seventh grade when I realized for the first time that things were not getting better; in fact, they were about to get much worse. All three of us were in band and as I was getting ready for a concert one night, Regina told me to wear one thing and I wanted to wear something else. She threatened to tell Daddy that I was arguing with her and when she did, he started cussing and yelling at me. When I tried to explain the situation, he punched me in the mouth. Daddy's fist was huge and I was a little girl of twelve, so the damage he did to my mouth with one hit was pretty painful. The shock that he had actually punched me outweighed the physical pain though. I was used to verbal abuse from him, but this was the first time he hit me.

I was still in shock when I got to the concert and I couldn't play my clarinet right. I was really upset and the principal asked me what was wrong. He was a nice man, so I told him what happened. Unfortunately, he was on friendly terms with my dad and didn't take me seriously. In fact, he told Daddy what I had said and, as soon as we were in the car, he threatened me. He said, "Don't you EVER tell anyone what goes on in our house again. What happens in this house stays in this house. It's our business and they can't do anything about it anyway." I was terrified. Daddy was a huge man and he had already given me a small taste of what he was capable of. He often reminded us that without him we had no other place to go for help.

From that time on, it was like a demon in him was let loose. He became a living nightmare of physical and verbal abuse. Many times when we argued with him or got in trouble, he put us out. We asked him why he acted that way and he said that it was the only way he could get through to us *#&*$#, because we didn't understand normal English. Thankfully, I had a cousin who lived a couple doors down, so we ran over there if we needed an escape. We jumped around to different places, staying with relatives and friends for small periods of time, but we always ended up back with Daddy.

Regina wasn't out of harm's way either. We often heard her screaming in the middle of the night and we'd run downstairs to try and defend her from Daddy so she wouldn't get hurt as bad. Each time we called the police, they made him leave for twenty-four hours, but each time he came home, he was just as arrogant as before. The only way she could protect herself for good was to get a restraining order against him, but she didn't do it.

There were times we came home from school to find patches of Regina's hair all over the house because they had been fighting. Her social outlet and stress relief was gambling, and Daddy accused her of using him and his money. She had her own job and used her own money, but he didn't want to hear that. It was easier for him to have an excuse to beat on her.

By this time, they slept in different rooms. My sisters and I never slept well, because we were always afraid he would come home drunk and ready to fight. We were up in the attic, so we were on edge all the time, never knowing if we would have to defend ourselves against him. Running wasn't an option, because he blocked our way to the stairs. One night we heard Regina screaming over and over for him to stop. The sound shot terror through us and when my sisters and I ran downstairs, we saw Daddy literally trying to fold her into the couch. He had hired a friend to spy on her and didn't like what his friend reported. Adriana and I jumped on him, trying to get him off of her, but we weren't any more effective than rag dolls. Eventually, he got tired and went into another room. From that point on, we resented Regina, because we realized that while we tried to help her as much as possible, she never did the same for us. We decided if she wasn't going to help us fight against him, then she was on her own. We were done.

Ayisha and Regina got into it a lot, too. She didn't like having to take care of us and let us know it. One day she heard Ayisha say something on the phone that she didn't like and started provoking Ayisha. She said, "You should put a sock in your mouth for saying things like that." At that point, she actually tried to stuff a sock in Ayisha's mouth. Ayisha kept batting her hand away and Regina started poking at Ayisha's forehead, saying, "Come on, what are you gonna to do about it? Fight me. Come on, what's wrong? Get up and fight."

At this point, Regina hit Ayisha and got completely out of control. I pulled her back onto the coffee table and it broke, then both of us were fighting with her. Daddy heard all the noise from the other room and ran in, yelling "What the &*$#@ is going on in here?!?" Regina told him we had attacked her, not telling the real story. He made us pack our bags and put us out of the house before we had a chance to explain our side of it. Now we would walk around outside with no place to go. I hated the humiliation he put us through.

Since he knew we didn't have any place to go and no one wanted us, he always taunted us, threatening to kick us out of his house. He told us that without him we'd be nothing, and that we were worthless trash who needed him. One of his favorite things to say was, "Don't bite the hand that feeds you." He said all we did was eat, sleep and push out sh&@#. He actually believed he was teaching us how to do things the right way by putting us down.

Every time he threatened to put us out, I felt my stomach twist in dread. I pictured myself on the streets, begging for food from wherever I could find it, stealing it if I had to. I imagined my sisters and I alone in the world without a soul to love us and take care of us, jumping from place to place just to get shelter for a night. Daddy didn't know just how much his words tore at my insides. He knew it got to all three of us, but the depth of the pain it caused was lost even to him.

At times, Adriana got the verbal abuse the worst. Since she didn't look like Ayisha and I, she had always felt a little bit like an outsider. When she was younger, she had serious asthma and had to be put on steroids for it. It caused weight gain that never went away, so she was bigger than us. Daddy always made fun of her weight, telling her she'd end up just like our mama and that she needed to stop eating so much. The truth was that Adriana ate less than Ayisha and I. She was a beautiful girl, but because of all the things he said and because it was already hard being overweight as a teenager, she felt terrible about herself and dressed in baggy clothes, not wearing make-up or drawing attention to herself. Daddy made it clear that he thought overweight girls and women were disgusting and lazy. In his way of thinking, he believed if he told her things like that, she would do something to make herself lose the weight, but she couldn't and he would not consider that. It was easier to rip her apart than to be sensitive enough to see the truth. Every day she heard the same things from him, over and over until it became the voice she heard in her head, telling her what she began to believe was the truth about her.

Unfortunately, after awhile all three of us started believing the things he said. If he said it that much, it must have been true. We resented him, because we knew he was partly right – we didn't have anyplace to go. We even had to beg Regina to ask Daddy for money for us, because he wouldn't give it to us if we asked him ourselves. We were so afraid of him that we used her as our main form of communication. He had a trigger that could go off at anytime, but we also had needs that had to be met. If we could have avoided dealing with him, we would have.

Life was a nightmare day after day. We had been yanked out of our comfortable, almost perfect home with a mother who pampered us. Now we had to fight for even the smallest rights. All that we had known from childhood was gone as if an invisible hand had come and erased it, leaving behind only a shadow of what had been. We never knew if we were going to wake up fighting for our lives, or if the day would find Daddy sober and reasonable, but somehow we knew we had to survive.

Daddy was a steady alcoholic and I got used to the stench of his breath after he'd been drinking. That smell matched the foulness of his moods. I couldn't imagine one without the other. It was a bitter, foul smell along with the stink of his body, as if the alcohol and been put in through his mouth, then released through every pore of his body. Being anywhere close to him was the last thing I wanted.

He was a walking disease and I had to fight between the hatred of this alcoholic and the desire to love a father I really didn't know.

At night, I sometimes imagined things the way they used to be. I'd see myself baking next to Mama, or hear her singing the good morning song again. I replayed every detail of the trips we went on and imagined the sound of our laughter. I tried to get lost in those moments, but as soon as sleep came, the nightmares began.

The terror of my home life affected every part of me. My stomach was always in knots, because I constantly imagined Daddy's footsteps coming toward me, ready to attack. Sometimes it wasn't my imagination, and he really was drunk and ready to hurt me. My heart ached, remembering how much Mama loved us and built us up, making us feel beautiful. With Daddy, I felt disgusting and worthless. I had to hide behind a mask of confidence when I was at school so no one would really see what I thought I was – what Daddy had convinced me I was. Trash – worthless, pathetic trash. It tore me up every minute of every day and I felt so lost. My sisters were my only steady ground and even we ripped each other apart.

When we were in eighth grade, we experienced the first life-threatening scene with Daddy. Ayisha was always the cleanest one of us and had cleaned our area upstairs, but by the time she came home from school, Adriana and I had messed it up. Ayisha was mad and threatened to tell Daddy. We told her to go ahead, but unfortunately, he was drunk – and our dad was a six-foot, four-inch mean drunk. She went to tell him about our mess and he accused her of starting problems. She was the boldest one of us, so often she took the worst of the abuse, but she definitely wasn't the problem. He started cussing her out and telling her to go back where she came from. As she started going back upstairs, he grabbed her by the hair and yanked her down, shouting, "Where the *&@#$ do you think you're going, you &*^&%!?!" By this time she was fighting back, but was no match for Daddy. He threw her around like she was weightless. She might as well have been a lifeless doll for all the effort it took him to throw her. The harder she fought, the worse it got. At one point, he had her on the futon and was choking her. Adriana and I pounded on him, fighting him with all our might, knowing as we did that he could turn his rage on us at any second, but she was our sister. Even if he killed us while we tried to defend her, we had to try. Adriana and I both jumped on him from the back and tried to get him away from her, but we were useless. No matter how hard we fought, his rage was a monster that kept feeding itself. Three young girls had no chance against it.

Every time he hit her, it felt as if he was hitting me. Triplets often say they can feel it when the other one is experiencing something. It's true. When one of my sisters was going through something, I felt it. As I watched Daddy beating Ayisha and watched her struggle for her life, it was as if it was me being punched, dragged and strangled. It was me, through her, fighting for my life. That made me try harder to rescue her from him. She was part of me and what happened to her, happened to me, too. I realized how hopeless it was – I couldn't do anything to help her, but I had to try.

Ayisha finally got away for a minute and ran into the kitchen to grab a knife. When Daddy saw that, he really lost it. He started yelling, "You trying to kill me? You want me dead?" and threw her against the refrigerator, where all the stuff that was on top fell on her. By that time he had ripped her Mickey Mouse sweatshirt from the shoulder all the way across.

I tried to call the police, but he ripped the phone out of the socket. Finally, I managed to reach them from a different phone, but when they came, I found out they weren't going to help us either. Regina always stayed on a different floor when Daddy was "disciplining" us and when the police came, she took his side.

A police man and woman came to our house. Daddy made us go upstairs so they wouldn't see us, but the man told him to bring us down. He asked Daddy if he had been drinking and he said he'd had a couple beers. That was as good as the situation got. As soon as Daddy told the man that he used to be a police officer, they started telling police stories, talking about where they worked, who they knew, and in a minute, they sounded like old friends.

In the meantime, the woman had gotten some story from Daddy about how we were being disrespectful and he was disciplining us. She started lecturing us about teenagers these days thinking they run the world and needing to be taken down a level. My sister had just about lost her life and this woman came at us with an arrogant, aggressive attitude. Then she pulled her own personal issues into it. She told us about her own daughter who was our age and had to be taken down a few notches. This woman who should never have been allowed onto the police force took Daddy's side and said we needed some good discipline. I hated to think of what her daughter went through. The woman was boldly disrespecting us and there was nothing we could do about it. Ayisha was desperate for help and tried showing the woman the ugly marks on her neck from where Daddy had strangled her, but the woman said those could have been from something else. No matter what we said, she stubbornly stuck to her attitude and belief that we deserved what we got.

The officers left without even doing a report. Any trust we had in the police force being there to protect us died right then. I can't imagine how many kids lose their lives daily because those in authority aren't doing their jobs, or don't want to be bothered with paperwork. Our hope died with our trust and respect. We were the only ones who would even try to protect each other and ourselves, yet the scene we had just gone through with Daddy showed us that we didn't have a chance. My fear now had another companion – hopelessness.

Daddy sat down on the couch, relaxed, and bragging about how he had gotten off and how no one was going to bring him down. We felt a mix of helplessness and rage. We wondered if anyone would protect us or if the struggle to survive was ours alone. I still wonder how many kids are in abusive homes and left there because the adults they go to for help either don't believe them, or don't want to deal with another kid in the state system.

Our great aunt hadn't passed away yet, so we went over to her house. Mama came and took Ayisha to the hospital. Daddy had choked her so hard that an infection started in her throat. Our aunt called Daddy and told him never to touch us like that again. Unfortunately, we were sent back to him and he told Ayisha it wouldn't happen again, but then made excuses for what he'd done, putting it all back on us. If we'd do what we needed to do, if we respected him more, if . . . if . . . if – and those ifs all ended up in his actions being our fault. It was years later, after some deaths in his family, that he finally apologized for what he'd done. His anger was like a spreading cancer and we were the ones who had to face it, desperately wanting someone to rescue us, but believing that no one would.

Every night after that I replayed that terrible night over and over in my mind, often imagining different ways it could have played out. I wondered if things would have gone differently if I'd had a knife under my pillow, or if it had been me instead. I had horrible nightmares about him succeeding in killing one of us while the other two watched helplessly. In my dreams I could hear those heavy footsteps coming up the stairs, my ears constantly straining toward the sound so I would be ready. But when reality came and the dreams faded, I knew there was nothing I could do. It was a terrible feeling; helplessness in the face of this man who held our very lives in his hands.

Chapter Five

The Story of Noah

More Than a Conqueror

Noah

Chapter 5 – More Than a Conqueror

"Yet in all these things we are more than conquerors through Him who loved us"

(Romans 8:37).

Noah's biological parents' rights were terminated when he was five years old. He was passed between relatives and state facilities until he was eight. A couple who wanted to adopt a little boy fell in love with Noah and brought him into their family, even going so far as to rename him after the adoptive father. Noah loved these people and did everything he could to make them love him. Unfortunately, so many things had happened to him when he was small that a lot of times his anger got the best of him and he had outbursts, usually breaking things.

Finally, after several years of this, his adoptive parents decided they couldn't handle him anymore and placed him in a residential home, hoping the staff there could teach him how to behave better. Noah was hurt and angry from what felt like rejection from a second set of parents. He acted up often for the staff at the facility and cried with promises that he would do better. He pleaded with them not to leave him there – that he wanted to come home. They kept telling him that his behavior just wasn't good enough.

One of the staff began to sit in on the meetings with his parents and started seeing where some of the problems came from. Noah's adoptive dad commented regularly on how stupid Noah was and his mother stopped coming, sending him letters about how she couldn't stand to see him like that. The staff member watched Noah's reactions to these things. A normally very outspoken boy sat with his head down and tears streaming down his face, believing every word his parents said was true.

One day she decided it was time to speak up. She said, "I have watched Noah over these past months and you should be ashamed of yourselves for talking about him this way. He has shown strength very few kids could show after being given to strangers by two sets of parents. Over these past months he has learned to open up, how to control his temper more often, and how to reason with people. He is one of the smartest kids I've ever seen. He can do things with electronics that engineers would be jealous of. He knows more facts than any kid his age would know if he wasn't so smart. Instead of tearing him down all the time, I think he deserves to have us give him a little praise."

It was the first time in his life that Noah felt an adult really believed in him. Noah's adoptive parents ended up giving him to the state, but he held onto the one person who thought he could make it. Because of her words, Noah is now a very successful electrical engineer. The odds were against him, but he kept fighting – he was determined that if one person thought he could do it, maybe he could. He chose to ignore the other voices that were saying he was worthless and instead, focused on the one who said he would make it.

Chapter 5 – More Than a Conqueror

I managed to hide our home life from our friends, but one day when two of them were at our house after school, they got a firsthand picture of our lives. I was working on a school project and writing a letter to Oprah, telling her about my life and hoping for some encouragement from her. I knew how many people she had helped and wanted to hear her say that what my sisters and I were going through didn't have to be the end of the story – that we could become something great. As I wrote it, I pictured my sisters and I in a different place, one where we were on top, one where we were safe and loved, and could do anything we set our minds to. I could see myself as a grown woman, successful and triumphant as a survivor of all I had been through, looking back on my life and saying, "See, you told me I wouldn't make it, but here I am – look at me now."

I was lost in the letter when Daddy came home drunk. He started trying to humiliate us in front of our friends. Ayisha said something in response to him and he accused her of talking back then made a threatening movement toward us. We were on our feet faster than he could have said "boo" and, as soon as we were up, he started chasing us around the table. We ran from him as though we were running for our lives, which was more true than our friends realized.

Our friends were terrified. They didn't know what to do. Thankfully, they got sent home soon after it started, so they didn't have to see any more. At school they told us they understood now what we were going through, but it was too late – we were humiliated that other people knew what our lives were like. My sisters and I just wanted to be normal kids, but that didn't seem possible for us.

At school, our teachers started noticing how much Ayisha and I cried in class. I was always looking over my shoulder, convinced that someone was always there, ready to destroy me. Between fear of Daddy and worry about Mama, I never got to just relax and let my guard down. It affected every part of my life. I couldn't have normal relationships, focusing in class was impossible, and work suffered. My mind raced so hard and so fast that I was exhausted all the time, always preparing for the next fight or the worst news. I was in survival mode every minute of every day.

Due to our breakdowns in class and the trouble Ayisha and I both had functioning, we were sent to the guidance counselor often. She was a young woman named Ms. Adams. Daddy had threatened us so many times about telling anyone what went on at our house, that for awhile I refused to open up to her. I knew how serious he was and how dangerous he would be if I disobeyed him. Ms. Adams was an angel of a woman and it was a huge struggle to keep myself in check and not pour everything out to her. I wanted to so much, but I was afraid. She didn't give up. She knew something was really wrong when two girls from the same family were unable to function in class and broke down regularly. Adriana had the least physical abuse, but the emotional abuse Daddy put her through was constant. All three of us had to deal with our own demons brought about by the man who was supposed to protect us. Between the reality of dealing with him and the cruelty of our imaginations, we were never safe and I longed to have someone fighting for me, someone who would take me seriously and step up in my defense.

Ms. Adams continued having us come see her and eventually I started opening up, because it felt so good to have someone genuinely care about what happened to me. Even as I talked, part of me questioned whether she was really as safe as she seemed. My experience had taught me that very few people should be trusted. The only ones in my world who I knew would be there for me were my sisters. Letting Ms. Adams into my world was both terrifying and soothing at the same time. It felt like an infection that I'd had for years was finally being released and receiving care. It was painful, but pressure was being let out. I didn't know what she would do with the information I gave her, but I desperately needed someone fighting for me, showing me compassion and love. My world was cruel, and having this woman genuinely seem to care was like finding water in a desert.

Unfortunately by this time, my sisters and I thought being choked and beat on was normal. We believed we had done things to get ourselves punished that way and that Daddy was justified in treating us like that. I fell into the lie that somehow I deserved it. As we told Ms. Adams our inner thoughts and fears, she told us over and over that Daddy's actions weren't okay and that nothing we did could ever deserve that.

After talking with us for awhile, she had the school police officer ask us some questions. Finally, she had enough information to hotline Daddy. The state workers came to investigate our house and looked to see if there were signs of neglect – did we have enough food, clothing, bedding, etc. Unfortunately for us, this made Daddy even more mad. He threatened that if we ever involved anyone else in our business again, we'd pay. He'd told us enough times before that we'd better not be spreading family business. I only realized years later that when someone says that, it usually means a whole lot of things are going on in the family that shouldn't be.

The state did their investigation, but nothing came of it. We continued opening up to Ms. Adams, because we felt safe with her. She kept documents of what we told her and with each incident, the case against our dad became more solid.

During my junior high years, I was experiencing something completely separate from Daddy's rage. People who talk about raising children always say that unless they are taught something different, they will model their parents. My downfall in that area was with boys.

Our parents were not married, and Mama was a classic case of a woman who "looked for love in all the wrong places." Before Daddy came along, my mother had been engaged twice. The first man was a crack addict and the other one just didn't work out. Her trend of choosing the wrong men and looking for love from people who didn't return it, or abused it, was normal.

We were used to different men coming to the house and spending the night. Mama told us they were "fixing the house up." I didn't know what was really happening until one night at the age of seven or eight when my sister was sick. I walked in while Mama and one of her male visitors were in bed together. I started screaming at them, cursing and throwing things, and Mama told me to go back upstairs. I was devastated. Suddenly, my view of my mother changed completely. I couldn't look at her the way I had anymore, because in that moment I lost so much respect for her. I didn't understand at the time that it was just one of the many ways she showed how little respect she had for herself.

Through all her other empty relationships, she never got over Daddy. In spite of the fact that she had left him, she kept trying to win back the man who had been responsible for leaving her to raise three children on her own. I could never understand why she tried so hard for someone who didn't love her or want her. I also didn't know how a woman who had grown up with an alcoholic father could allow herself to get involved in a romantic relationship with an alcoholic man. It made no sense to me, but as I got older I realized it was, because that was familiar to her. She knew what alcoholism was all about and it was comfortable.

There was a time Daddy came to the house at midnight and when I asked Mama why he was there, she said, "I'm trying to win your father back." My sisters and I were angry with him for the pain he put her through, but we were also angry with her because she allowed him to use her.

Chapter Six

The Story of Sharone

Looking For Love in All the Wrong Places

Sharone

Chapter 6

Looking For Love in All the Wrong Places

"Above all else, guard your heart, for it is the wellspring of life" (Proverbs 4:23).

"Flee from sexual immorality. All other sins a man commits are outside his body, but he who sins sexually sins against his own body"

(1 Corinthians 6:18).

Sharone was twelve years old when her mother died suddenly of a stroke. Even though she was the middle child, her brothers and sisters looked to her for direction. She believed she had to be strong for them. She started making money by getting involved with gangs and drugs, and believed survival was only possible if she kept herself tough and distant.

She and her brother and sister were sent to live with their dad, a man they hardly knew. Within seven months of her mama's death, Sharone's dad started molesting her. His girlfriend denied it and the court system let him go, telling him that he had to take classes to get his children back, but she and her siblings were placed in residential programs. She put on a tougher front, believing if the justice system wasn't even going to help her, she had to help herself.

She went on weekend visits to her dad's house and often came back to the children's home drunk or high, but she soon found out her tough shell couldn't stand up to everything.

Several of the staff realized quickly that she had amazing potential. She was a natural leader and was gifted in music and rap. Unfortunately, she had a lot of baggage to get past before her potential could be reached. Every day and night they worked with her, finally getting her to open up and even cry. But she still fought to keep the walls.

The real part of her wanted out of the prison she was in, but she was so afraid that if she let herself be vulnerable, she would be abused again. Besides, she was used to the hard life – it was comfortable for her.

She was placed in a foster home and soon began attending church with one of the staff she had known before. She realized she had a decision to make. God was actively pursuing her and she felt a pull toward Him, but the world still had a strong hold on her.

Finally, she gave her life to Jesus Christ, letting Him win the tug-of-war for her soul. She hadn't known before that she could have real joy. She thought it was going to be a miserable life of fighting all the time, but with Him, she had hope, peace and love that went beyond anything she'd ever known.

Now Sharone is working on a Gospel rap CD, performing at Christian events and understanding that God was holding His hand out to her the whole time – waiting for her to come to Him and experience what life could really be like. Sharone reaches out to teens and adults around her, telling them how she used to be and letting them see the difference in her now. Through her story and life, many others are finding out that they don't have to be stuck in a prison of pain forever – they, too, can experience freedom.

Chapter 6

Looking For Love in All the Wrong Places

Mama did everything she could to win Daddy's heart. She thought if he was around, it would help lighten her load. Instead, he only broke her down more. He promised that he loved her and would marry her, but they were empty words and she finally realized he was using her for his own pleasures. He had no intention of taking responsebility for us or being there for her. She was left with three babies and a broken, empty heart. She was in and out of relationships all the time, but she never got married.

Daddy wasn't a man who committed to any woman. While he was with my mother, he always had other women on the side. He didn't take responsibility for raising any of his children. Mama was the only one who took him to court for child support. He even went so far as to deny that we were his.

Needless to say, I didn't have a healthy understanding of how relationships between men and women were supposed to work. Like my mother before me, I believed my need for love could be filled by a man – at that time, a boy. Mama actually encouraged us to get involved with boys.

No one had taught me anything about my body or sex. My parents were not a good example and I had no idea about things like intimacy, real love, or my body as a sacred gift of God. I had no morals, because I had never been taught to have morals. I believed I could do whatever I wanted with my body because it was mine. Besides, if a boy really loved me, wasn't it the right thing to let him have my body? That's what I believed at the time.

I was thirteen when I had my first "real" boyfriend, who was fifteen. I thought he was wonderful, especially because he always told me he loved me. That was enough to make me weak when I should have been strong. His mother grew up with an alcoholic father, so she understood me and became a mentor, inviting me to the house a lot. I looked up to her.

My friends all pressured me to have sex with him and I decided that my birthday gift to him would be to give him my virginity. I thought my friends knew what they were talking about, but I didn't find out until later that none of them had been sexually active and didn't have a clue what it was really like. They coached me on what to do and say, how to look, everything. By this time I was fourteen and he was sixteen.

The plan was that while his family was at the park for a family reunion, he and I would be at his house. I learned quickly that everything my friends said was a lie. My first sexual experience was painful and nothing like they described it. In addition to the pain was the humiliation.

Everyone came back to the house early because it began storming. My boyfriend had locked all the doors and taken the key from his mom's key ring in case they came home. As soon as we heard them trying to get in, we raced to put our clothes on, but the embarrassment was already there. When his mama saw him half naked, she asked what we'd been doing. His aunt found a condom wrapper and pulled us into another room to talk to us about what it means to be sexually active. She said she wouldn't tell his mother, but that it was better if we didn't do that anymore. His cousin, who was a virgin, encouraged us to abstain, but we didn't listen.

I stayed with him until my freshman year, but started cheating on him with a football player. It was a game for us both. The football player had a girlfriend and I had a boyfriend, so we did our best to sneak around. I was sexually active with both of them and both said they loved me.

I could relate more to the football player, because both his parents were alcoholics and they let me go to their house anytime I wanted. My other boyfriend's life was more ideal than mine and he was more reserved. The football player was a thug, a jock, and really fine, so all the girls wanted him. Each of them made me feel different. By this time I enjoyed sex and liked the thrill of not getting caught.

The football player hadn't told me he had STDs and when I found out he'd passed them on to me, I left him alone. My boyfriend left me because he found out about the cheating and STDs, and didn't want anything to do with me. His mother turned on me and my parents, and his sisters were calling me any name they could think of for a loose woman. Daddy even started calling me a wild animal. On top of that, I knew something was going wrong in my body and when Mama took me to the gynecologist, I felt humiliation like I'd never felt before.

I sat alone waiting for the doctor to come in. My heart was beating hard, because I didn't know what to expect and I never imagined I would be in this place. The room around me was so sterile and impersonal, but what I was dealing with sunk its claws into my inner core, rotting me from the inside out. As I sat on the examination table, I made a promise to God. I said that as long as I didn't have AIDS or something serious, I would dedicate my body to Him until I got married.

The doctor came in and ran some humiliating tests on me, then explained STDs in detail. The more he said, the dirtier I felt. As soon as I got home, I went into the shower and scrubbed so hard that it's a miracle my skin didn't come off. By God's grace the antibiotics took care of the STDs, but they didn't take away the rest of my problems. Natural consequences were always something that applied to other people, not to me – until then.

My reputation at school was terrible. All the words used for an easy girl got tagged onto me. Just about everyone knew I had STDs and who I had gotten them from. Mama got drunk and called everyone, telling them about my doctor visit and the outcome. I was so angry and humiliated that I promised myself I would never confide in her again. I had lost all respect for myself by this time, too.

In spite of that, I stayed true to my word that I

wouldn't have sex again until my wedding night. My physical purity began in December, 1997. At first I didn't even want to be in another relationship because of all the information I had gotten on STDs. Unfortunately, my desire for love was stronger than my fear of what could happen, so I continued getting in relationships, but wouldn't give in to the pressures for sex. I won't lie; it wasn't easy for me to stop, but I had gotten scared enough of what could happen to me that it overshadowed my desire.

A major temptation came for me when I was a freshman. This boy started taking me to church with him. He was involved in ministry, looked like he was the greatest Christian around, but in reality he was a wolf in sheep's clothing. About six months into our relationship, he started pressuring me to have sex. His reasoning was that we were going to get married anyway, so it was okay in God's eyes. By the time I told my best friend that I had decided to go ahead and do it, she told me not to because he was cheating on me with her sister. At that point, I started believing all Christians were hypocrites. If they were all going to look good but have a hidden agenda, I didn't want anything to do with them.

I continued getting into relationships, sometimes

just so I could say I had someone. Most of the guys I dated had backgrounds like mine, so they understood where I was coming from. I wanted to feel loved and thought they were the answer.

Through all this, people assumed I was sexually active because I was with so many different guys, but the truth was that most of them broke up with me because I wouldn't sleep with them. I had between ten and twelve boyfriends during my teenage years, and all of them left me feeling empty – wanting something I couldn't name and that they couldn't fill.

Looking back on it now, I wish someone had told me how beautiful I was in God's eyes and to hold onto my body as my most precious treasure, and avoid temptation that comes from relationships with guys who don't look at sexual purity in the same way. My intentions to stay pure after my STDs were sincere, but I put myself into situations that God alone rescued me from. I also continued feeling empty, grasping for something deeper than what any person could give me.

Chapter Seven

The Story of Carly

A Ray of Hope

Carly

Chapter 7 – A Ray of Hope

"'For I know the plans I have for you,' declares the Lord, 'plans to prosper you and not to harm you, plans to give you hope and a future'"

(Jeremiah 29:11).

Carly was thirteen years old and living with her mother and four brothers when her life changed. Her mother was a single parent who worked all the time just to meet their basic needs. She wasn't home much, so the kids had lots of freedom – too much freedom. They were all close in age, so it made sense that they had some of the same friends. Since Carly was the only girl, she got a lot of attention from her brothers' friends, especially when they were over at her house.

Andre was the only one who caught her attention. It wasn't long before Andre, two years older than

Carly, convinced her to have sex with him. At first it was an adventure, then an addiction. Carly never felt good about herself, but the physical pleasure always won out in the end.

After a few months, Carly started noticing changes in her body. Her periods were starting to skip, she was hungry or sick all the time, and she felt terrible. If that weren't enough, her private area was so uncomfortable that she cried herself to sleep sometimes. Finally, in a rare moment when her mother was home, Carly told her about it. Her mother began to cry and went straight for the phonebook to call a doctor.

After doing some tests, the doctor confirmed that not only was Carly pregnant, but she had several STDs. The doctor hotlined her mother, thinking it might be a situation of neglect. The investigation was dropped when they learned that she was only gone during the days, but Carly's mother knew something had to be done.

Carly was checked into a crisis pregnancy facility where she could stay for the duration of her pregnancy, then for a year after the baby was born. The main concern was whether the baby would make it with all the STDs that were in its mother's body.

With a lot of discomfort, regret and tears, Carly carried the baby and the baby was born three months early. The carefree teenager Carly had been disappeared as she watched her baby struggle for life every day for four months. Reality began to hit her that life would never be the same again. She had messed up.

Carly is now twenty-eight years old with a fourteen-year-old daughter. Her daughter has suffered from all kinds of health problems because she was so premature, and the phone is always ready in case 911 needs to be called. Carly looks back on her life with regret; not only for herself, but for her daughter. Due to her choices, she has had to watch her daughter struggle and knows she always will.

She has tried to teach her daughter the things she learned from her own mistakes. If her daughter listens to her rather than following her example, there can be hope, but if her daughter follows in her footsteps, Carly knows only pain is ahead for them.

Chapter 7 – A Ray of Hope

The Department of Family Services continued investigating our family situation, and the teachers and administrative staff at school were supportive. They didn't believe Ayisha when she made up stories about falling down stairs or tripping on something each time she showed up with bruises or cuts, and because of that, we ended up with more support than we would have otherwise.

The teachers were all kind to us. Everyone knew what our lives were like and it was humiliating, especially because we were popular at school. The worst times were when Mama called the school while she was drunk. She was an alcoholic and couldn't hide it from anyone. All we wanted to do was crawl into a cave where only the three of us could go and hide away until the shame passed. Most of the time we could pretend everything was okay while we were with our friends doing school activities, but when we got slapped right in the face by our parents openly showing their behavior, there wasn't anything we could do about it.

We called our principal "Pa-Pa", because he always let us stay in his office for a while when we were having a hard time in class. He gave us candy and encouraged us.

Things continued to get worse, but one night Daddy went so far that even he couldn't get away with it. I was at the mall after school looking for a homecoming dress, and I was going to meet Adriana and Ayisha at home after I was done. When Ayisha got home she saw that Daddy was passed out from drinking. She hated both Daddy and Regina by that time, and just looked at him with disgust.

Regina had been cooking for him all day and left a pile of dishes in the sink. She started giving Ayisha a hard time about washing them up. She said that if she didn't do them, she'd wake Daddy up and see if she would still refuse. Ayisha ignored her and went upstairs because she was tired.

Next thing she knew, Daddy was in our room, yelling and cussing, asking her why she didn't do the #$%*& dishes. He shouted at her to get her lazy @#&# up, go downstairs and get them done. Ayisha got up and went to her sock drawer, because Regina didn't want us in the kitchen without socks or house shoes. Daddy went back downstairs and she continued looking for socks. When he came back upstairs demanding to know why she wasn't doing what he'd told her to, she tried to explain, but he yelled that she was lying and threw an Algebra book at her head. Then he attacked her and when she fell on the bed, he started punching her and trying to smother her with a pillow.

By this time I was home. Adriana and I ran upstairs to try and stop him, but we couldn't. Ayisha's head hit the side of the bed and in the mirror, she could see blood running down her face. Finally, she got away and ran down the stairs, but he was right behind her. She saw a butcher knife on the counter that Regina had been using earlier, but when Daddy saw her holding it, he got even more out of control. He grabbed the trash can and hit her in the head. She fell against the refrigerator and I called the police while Adriana continued doing what she could to get him away from Ayisha. Daddy started dragging Ayisha around the house by her hair and just then Regina came in. He stopped beating on Ayisha, but told her to get the *&@@$ out of his house.

The police showed up soon. Due to our past experiences, my sisters and I believed they couldn't be trusted and wouldn't do anything to help, but calling them seemed to be the only option. Daddy was already sitting in the living room, legs crossed and arms spread out over the back of the couch as if he owned the world.

This time Daddy was obviously drunk and Ayisha was a beaten mess. The police chief asked him what had happened and Daddy wouldn't give him a straight answer. Finally, he said that Ayisha had fallen down the stairs, and that she'd given him an attitude and said, "Punk, I ain't doin' no dishes." Realistically, we were all so afraid of Daddy that those words would never have come from any of us.

This was the first officer who didn't believe Daddy's lies or take his side. This man didn't say we deserved what we got and he didn't pat our father on the back for "disciplining" us. He asked us if there was anywhere we could go for the night and we thought of our friend Tim, who was like an older brother to us. Tim came to get us and the next day at school, Adriana and I were called into the main office. The principal, security guard and school counselor were there waiting for us.

Ayisha hadn't come to school because her mouth was hurting so bad. Ms. Adams called her at Tim's house and Ayisha told her why she wasn't there. Ms. Adams told her she was concerned and asked her to come to the school so she could talk to her. Once Ayisha came, they took us into a more private area and told us they couldn't send us back home.

The police took us to the juvenile facility and we stayed there for the night, scared and wondering what was going to happen to us. We found out that our aunt was the only one willing to take all three of us, but when the state inspected her home and realized she didn't have enough space, Ayisha and I were removed from there and told we would be in foster care.

The thought of living with complete strangers, away from all our friends and all that was familiar was scary enough, but the worst part was that we would be separated. Adriana was able to stay with our aunt, but Ayisha and I were put in different children's homes. The social worker who took on our case told us it was because they couldn't find a place that would take all three of us. However, we found out it was really because we argued too much and she didn't think we should be together. I had never been so scared in my life. Even though living with Daddy guaranteed fear every day, at least it was kind of predictable. I couldn't even guess what was going to happen to us now.

I was about to go through the biggest culture shock of my life. My home life was bad, but when I was at school I was involved in everything. It was an excuse to stay away from the house as much as possible, and to try and distract myself from what went on there. I was in cheerleading, student counsel, band and other activities. Daddy never came to any of my events, but while I was in those, I was safe. I had something to look forward to.

Suddenly, I was separated from my only support system – my sisters—and taken to a children's home where I was immediately treated as if I was a criminal rather than a victim. Everything that was familiar to me was stripped away. Before I could be put into the facility, I had to go through some medical tests. I was already scared, but now I had to get a physical, AIDS testing, hepatitis shots and other painful things. I felt violated, but I had no say in what happened to me – I was just another kid in the foster system.

Years later, I found out Daddy cried when he discovered we'd been removed from his home and put into facilities. Unfortunately, they weren't tears of regret, but tears of blame. He hated that we were in homes, but thought that if our mama had done what she needed to do and if we had been more grateful for his "discipline" and shut our mouths about it, the whole thing wouldn't have happened. I didn't understand until much later that my daddy was filled with guilt, but didn't know what to do about it. He was a wounded man who was unable to deal with his own pain, so his outlet was drinking, which turned into abuse. It was easier to dump his mess on everyone else than it was to accept and resolve it. I fully believe that when we first went to live with him, his intentions were to do the best for us, but he didn't know what it was like to be taken care of, and he didn't know how to do things right for his own kids.

Mama also blamed us. She said if we hadn't "chosen" to stay with Daddy, things would have been fine. Like Daddy, I think the guilt inside her was like a deadly cancer. It must have been a nightmare for her to realize that the thing she dreaded so much had happened: her alcoholic father turned his kids over to state custody and now she, also an alcoholic, had lost us to state custody. She had been raised in facilities and strangers' homes; now we were being raised in facilities and passed from one home to the next. She had to face herself every day. Once a woman who was an almost perfect mother, now a woman who had very little to claim as her own – a woman who could barely function in any area of her life. Yet she still loved us, which made it that much harder.

When I arrived at the children's home, I remember sitting at a round table in the intake office. I was in shock and felt withdrawn from the whole world. I was scared and alone, and had no idea what to expect. I had never been separated from my sisters before. I was angry and felt betrayed by my parents, but I also wanted to be with them, in spite of the abuse. They were my family and suddenly I felt like the only one on the face of the earth.

My case worker wasn't a compassionate woman and it felt like she labeled me based on what she read in my paperwork rather than seeing me for the scared girl that I was. It wasn't a good label either – I might as well have been a convict who deserved to be in a place like this.

The intake lady went over the rules and regulations of the home. She listed off who I could and couldn't talk to on the phone, who I could and couldn't see on visits, and I found out that because Ayisha was at another facility with different rules, I wouldn't be able to talk to her at all for awhile. My phone calls were limited to three ten-minute calls a week. Thankfully, I could talk to Adriana, and sometimes she put Ayisha and I on three-way.

My first placement at the children's home was in their temporary crisis area. The staff was nice enough, but the environment wasn't like anything I was used to. It was a military type of setting. Coming from a background with a lot of freedom to this strange new world was a nightmare. I was thrown in with other kids with unstable back-grounds, and wondered if it would have been better to stay with Daddy and deal with the abuse.

The pain in my heart was even worse, because the day after I arrived, the home had their big annual festival where lots of people from the community came to give donations and look around. They all looked so happy, almost like wax figurines. I wanted to get away from them all, but I couldn't. Even old residents came to visit again. I couldn't figure out what made them come back to this place, but there they were. Even that was painful. It was almost as if they were rubbing it in, telling me, "See, we got out. Don't you wish you could?"

It was a depressing environment, looking more like an institution than a home. The buildings were old and in desperate need of maintenance work. I didn't even want to take a shower without flip-flops on. Even though we had chores every day, the house never really looked clean.

Some of the rules in the cottage made no sense. We had to ask to cross every time we wanted to go from the hallway into the kitchen area or out into the common room. Even everyday needs like using the bathroom or getting something to drink or eat weren't allowed unless we asked first. It felt like a prison system. People kept telling us how lucky we were to even have shelter, a bed to sleep in and food to eat, and that we should be grateful. But our freedom had been stripped from us and we couldn't be thankful about that.

I felt bitterness grow in me every time one of the staff had the nerve to tell me what I should be feeling. They had no idea what it was like to be in my shoes, or else they would have kept their mouths shut. What did they know about having life as they knew it ripped from them without warning? Nothing. They didn't have a clue what I was going through and they never would.

For awhile when I first got there, I stayed in bed at night and cried for hours. I couldn't sleep and the only thoughts that went through my head were dark. I had been so active before that I didn't have time to think, but now it seemed that all I had was time to get sucked down into my pain. I was lonely and afraid, sleeping in a room with a stranger. Every night I wished for the day when they would take me out of there. I worried about my sisters, wondering if they were suffering as much as I was.

I wondered what the kids at my old school thought about Ayisha and I suddenly disappearing, but I was too embarrassed to let them know what really happened, so I told Adriana to make up stories about where Ayisha and I were. I had been popular in my old school, but now I tried to stay to myself as much as possible. I didn't stay in touch with my old friends because I was so ashamed.

Those were some of the darkest days of my life. I had never felt so lost. My whole identity had been taken away from me and I started seriously thinking about suicide. The thought often went through my head that I had no reason to live, and I started imagining myself not reaching age sixteen. I got lost in my own world and pictured myself stepping in front of a car and getting hit, or slitting my wrists or popping pills – anything to end the nightmare and loneliness I was in. Every dream and desire I had before faded away so that I went on shutdown. It was hard enough to put one foot in front of the other, so I refused to see beyond the day I was in. My real motivation for thinking of suicide was the thought that if I was gone, my parents would realize what a mess they had made of things, do what they needed to do, and put the family back together. Every time I sat in the dark thinking about suicide, a small whisper went through my heart, "Don't give up – I have a purpose for you." I didn't know what that whisper was yet, but it distracted me from my thoughts and brought me enough comfort to take one more breath; to walk one more step.

Chapter Eight

The Story of Latisha

From Victim to Victorious

Latisha

Chapter 8 – From Victim to Victorious

"Being confident of this very thing, that He who has begun a good work in you will complete it until the day of Jesus Christ" (Philippians 1:6).

Latisha was twenty-one years old when she became pregnant. It wasn't planned and she didn't want a baby messing up her plans, so she got an abortion. People had convinced her that it was her choice – that she didn't need that extra burden. It was just a piece of tissue growing inside her, not a life.

What they didn't tell her was the agony she would go through during the procedure, or that she could have complications later on, or that she would lie awake at night thinking she heard a baby crying.

For several months she suffered emotionally and mentally. She felt guilt that no one had warned her about. To top that off, she began to have physical problems. She found out that not all the tissue had been removed and it was now causing infection in her ovaries and uterus. The doctors tried to remove it, but it was too late. They said she would never be able to have children again. She was crushed. She wanted children – eventually. But she had wanted it her way – in her timing. Now it would never happen for her.

Latisha didn't have to struggle with that knowledge for long. Several weeks after she learned about the infection, she hemorrhaged. She was too weak to get to a phone and she was by herself. By the time someone found her, it was too late.

Latisha thought her plans were the main priority and she thought she had "rights." The choices she made and the priorities she placed on top ended up not only killing her unborn child, but her as well. She never thought it would happen to her. She heard about it with other people, but thought she was above it. Latisha will never have another chance to fix what she did, but other women do. Many of Latisha's friends who had encouraged her to live her own life without the burden of a child have changed their minds. They are the first ones in the centers for abortion alternatives, helping women of all ages choose not to go through the same thing as Latisha.

Chapter 8 – From Victim to Victorious

Some days were good, but others were terrible. The staff was compassionate, but the nicer they were, the more I rebelled, because they weren't my family – they weren't the ones I wanted around me, giving me comfort. I didn't want to get close to anyone, partly because my experiences had taught me that people didn't stay around for long; either they or I would be gone any day. There were too many goodbyes and nothing was certain. It only took a second for everything to change.

I also decided that if my own family had hurt me so many times before, what would keep outsiders from being even worse? I might have come from a dysfunctional family, but no one could separate the bond I had with my sisters. They were the only people who were constant in my life and now they had been taken away from me. We had been together since we were fighting over space inside my mother. Being away from them felt as if two parts of me were ripped away – parts that kept me alive. My sisters were the only ones I trusted and the ones that motivated me to keep going. No matter what happened, we leaned on each other for strength and support. As long as we had each other, we knew we would be okay. Now my sisters, who I believed would be there no matter what, were gone. I had no guarantees in life anymore.

I was angry at the world and so I was determined to keep to myself, shutting everyone else out. For awhile I refused to build relationships with the girls who lived in the cottage with me. Those girls had plenty of issues of their own. My stuff was getting stolen and one of the girls was a bully. Since I was the oldest, she felt threatened by me and kept trying to pick fights. I wasn't willing to let her push me around, which made her mad. One time she took my shoes and threw them into the muddy yard, then denied it. All the girls knew about it, so she didn't get away with it. Another girl read my diary. The others thought that was funny, but since I put all my deepest thoughts and feelings into it, I felt violated. The deepest parts of my life that I wouldn't share with anyone else were in those books. It was my outlet. I felt as if they had ripped me to shreds and left pieces of me scattered on the ground, fully exposed. I told Mama about it, so she brought me a trunk with a lock on it so I could lock my diaries away.

Mama came to visit me at the home a few times and since her nickname for me was "Bunny," she usually brought a bunny of some kind for me. I could see that Mama was really trying to do better, but it haunted her that she had failed us in spite of the fact that she had tried so hard in our early years. I could see the look on her face every time she saw me – she hadn't done any better for us than her father had done for her – but she still loved me and that meant more to me than she knew. She went through AA classes and parenting classes, working hard, but each time she finished one thing, the state added another requirement.

Daddy continued to deny the abuse every time we had a court date. He felt he had done the best he could with us, but the court ordered him to go through anger management and parenting classes. He visited me a couple times, but every time either of my parents visited, it became that much harder to stay at a children's home. My heart broke when I had to say goodbye to them. No childhood dreams include mess and chaos. My reality was far from my dreams. Families aren't supposed to be separated by force, but mine was. I never knew if or when I would see Mama again. The anxiety that had torn at me so many times in the past was even worse, because now

I didn't have my sisters with me to lean on during the unknown times. I didn't know where Mama was when she wasn't with me.

Finally, I made one friend in the crisis unit. Her mom put her in because she was rebellious. I felt comfortable with her and we got close. After thirty days, she was removed. We stayed in contact for awhile after she left, but she started getting into trouble again and eventually I lost track of her. Another girl was there who had already had a baby who was living with her mother. My roommate was diagnosed as paranoid schizophrenic. I liked to keep things clean and she didn't. Every day was a battle, and it seemed as if I was thrown into a world that made no sense and was driven by chaos.

When I was first put into the facility, they told me I would only be there for a couple weeks, thirty days at the most. As long as I could look at it that way, it was easier. I had hoped that there would be an end to it. When it was obvious to everyone that I was seriously depressed, I had to go see a psychiatrist. I knew if I answered the questions honestly, he would put me on medication, so I lied to him, telling him everything was fine and that I was doing okay. I said I understood why I was there and that life was great. Apparently I lied well, because he didn't put me on medicine.

There were a couple adults that took a special interest in me while I was there. One of them, Ms. Tanya, knew I didn't really have anyone and the facility wouldn't allow me to get my hair permed or cut, so she took me on weekend outings to get my hair done and to get real food. I trusted her and opened up to her in a way I didn't with other staff. She always told me how special I was. She spent time with me and took me to do fun things. She was the closest thing I had to a mother figure at that point.

Another lady came along who made a difference for me. She was a white lady who volunteered to do a Bible study with us every Monday night. I remember her character more than anything. She had a beautiful spirit and when she asked if I wanted to give my life to Christ, I said yes, but that I didn't know what to do. She led me in prayer – I told Jesus I believed He had died on the cross for me and had risen again, that I knew I was a sinner and that He was the only one who could take the punishment for me, and that I wanted Him to be my Savior. I told Him that I knew I needed Him. She gave me a Bible, but I couldn't read very well and didn't understand what it was saying, so she offered to come every Thursday night to help me study Scripture. After awhile, her grandmother passed away and she stopped coming. I lost contact with her, but always remember her for the time she spent with me.

Even though I had given my life to Christ, I was still angry at God. I thought life was supposed to be easy once I became a Christian, but it wasn't. In fact, it seemed to get even harder. I was confused and became even more depressed. I didn't realize that there is an enemy and that Satan will do all he can to keep people from having a personal relationship with Jesus. I didn't know that he has no mercy. I tried listening to Gospel music to help lift me up, but I was still so lost.

Several of the staff members told me regularly that they saw something different in me and that I shouldn't be there. That didn't help. Of course, I shouldn't be there. No kid belongs in a children's home; they belong with two loving parents. What I didn't understand was that God had set me apart to be someone special for Him. That's what they saw in me.

One of the staff told me years later that she

remembered a night when I did devotions for the girls in the cottage. I told them that God had us there for a reason, and that even though we didn't under-stand it and thought it was the worst place in the world to be, one day we would be able to look back and see some good from it. The staff said she watched as the girls responded to what I said, and that somehow I was able to say it in a way they understood and accepted. At that point, she knew she was watching the beginnings of a natural teacher.

My outlook on life got worse when I found out the hope I had in only being there thirty days was gone. They moved me into the residential cottage, which meant they expected me to be there for awhile. I knew they could keep me there for a year. Every time a court date came, they told me I might be going home. Something always went wrong though, so I was on a constant roller coaster of hope and disappointment. I was so angry, because I thought the adults in my life weren't doing their part. I believed my parents weren't putting effort into getting us back like they should have, and the state case workers weren't filing papers like they were supposed to, so I suffered for it.

I was able to talk to my sisters on the phone, but

Ayisha couldn't have visits with me until three months after we'd been put into the homes. Our aunt brought Adriana to visit me, but I had to earn points to go on a weekend visit to see her. Those points were what I held onto. They equaled freedom. The more points I earned, the more freedom I had. I worked to stay on the highest point system, so I could have special privileges like walking to the mall nearby and working part time down in the dining room for the cook. The more points I earned, the more responsibility I was given. I wanted to succeed, so I worked hard and stayed out of trouble.

Chapter Nine

The Story of Stacy

You Can Make It

Stacy

Chapter 9 – You Can Make It

"Trust in the Lord with all your heart and lean not on your own understanding; in all your ways acknowledge Him, and He will make your paths straight" (Proverbs 3:5-6).

Stacy knew she wasn't the prettiest girl around. She tried to avoid looking at magazines or watching movies with supermodel actresses, because it only made her more aware of how different she was from them. The kids at school made fun of her and confirmed what she already believed about herself – that she was ugly. Because of that, she tried to stay away from the "popular" kids and surrounded herself with others that were similar to her. When she was with them, she didn't feel like she was so alone.

Stacy stuck with the same people all the way through junior high and high school. She was terrified about going to college, because those friends wouldn't be there. She was afraid the whole thing would start over and that she would be reminded all over again that she wasn't up there with America's most beautiful.

One of her professors in college loved group work and warned them at the beginning of the semester that most of the classes would be done in groups. Stacy thought her worst nightmare had come true. She tried to ignore the rude comments some of the little girls made within earshot or pretend the twisted looks the guys threw her way were directed toward someone else.

One day her roommate invited Stacy to a weekend retreat with their college group from church. Stacy was terrified, but her roommate was so encouraging that she agreed to go. The first night the group sat around the bonfire, singing songs and telling about things God had done in their lives.

When the leader stood up to speak, he put his notes to the side and said, "I had a devotional all planned out, but God has put something else on my heart. I believe this is for someone specific, but I have to let you know it's not a manly topic, so please understand that I'm not very comfortable saying this. Out of obedience, I need to."

For a moment he looked at each one of them, then said, "God wants me to tell you that you're beautiful. He knows the things other people look at to make judgments on beauty, but to Him, all those things are shallow and wasted. When He looks at you, He sees the heart of royalty. He sees a unique person that He handcrafted exactly the way He wanted you – and He enjoys gazing on the beautiful thing He created when He looks at you. No matter what others have said to you, no matter how you think you measure up in others' eyes, He wants you to know that their opinions don't matter anymore. The way He sees you is what counts."

For the first time in her life, as tears streamed down her face, Stacy felt truly, fully beautiful. She realized it wasn't about who had the best hair, figure or make-up. The beauty she had outran others by miles – she had beauty of the heart that came all the way to her smile. Once she started seeing herself through God's eyes, she became a whole new person. She began to reach out to others who were hurting and lonely, and as people saw her beauty, they were drawn to her like never before.

Today, Stacy is married to one of the most attractive men she has ever known, has three children and spends her days building others up so they, too, can hear and know the message that was given to her – God's scale of beauty far outweighs all the rest.

Chapter 9 – You Can Make It

When I first got put into the home, I went to school on campus, which was fine with me. It meant I didn't have to pretend or hide my embarrassment about being in a children's home. I was also behind academically, so the on-campus school was a better fit for me. When I moved to residential, I had to start at the public school nearby. It was awful, because I didn't know anyone and now I was the minority. The school I had been at was predominantly African American, but now that wasn't the case. It was a whole different world for me. The curriculum was also more advanced than where I had been before and I struggled. At my old school I was almost illiterate, but I always got out of reading out loud in class by acting out. I couldn't get away with that at my new school, so everyone knew I was having a hard time. The teachers knew where I lived and that I was one of the "children's home" kids, so they were really nice to me, but that didn't make it easier.

I didn't get involved in activities and I never told people where I lived. In fact, when the bus dropped me off, I waited until it rolled away before I walked across the street to my cottage. I always dreaded having to go back to the home, because the only common thread we all had was that our family lives had gone wrong somehow and now we were in a facility. Other than that, we were as different as night and day, yet were forced to live together.

The shame I felt at being fifteen years old and living in a children's home was terrible. It was proof that my life wasn't normal like everyone else's seemed to be. Either my parents or I had done something that put me there. I couldn't feel good about myself, because my life was being dictated to me by the system. I was at the mercy of everyone else, but had no voice of my own. It felt as though I was under a microscope and couldn't escape.

It was a few months into my time at the children's home when I really began to change. I no longer fought with people or got into trouble. I had a lot of time to think and began to realize that I didn't have anyone to lean on except God. That's when I really started to grow.

I wasn't suicidal anymore and the worst times were dealing with loneliness. In those times, I learned to allow God to fill my void and to lean on Him when I felt like I couldn't keep going.

By that time I was the oldest resident in the cottage and the other girls started looking up to me. I was a positive leader for them and found myself being shadowed by an eleven year old. The more my desire for Christ increased, the more I changed and became a better person. I wasn't afraid of people like I had been before and now I was more willing to reach out.

When I became a Christian, my mindset was that I wasn't going to make an empty commitment. If I was going to do this, I was going to do it all the way. I didn't want to give people room to call me a hypocrite. I had seen too many people say they believed in Jesus as their Savior, but as soon as things got tough, they bailed out. I didn't respect that, and I wasn't going to make the same mistake.

In spite of my growing relationship with God, I was still so disappointed every time I found out I didn't get to go home yet. There were times I was angry at Him, because I thought everything was supposed to get better once I gave my life to Him. But, my circumstances weren't changing. I even asked the question, "God if you really love me, then why is this happening?" I didn't realize it at the time, but He was taking me through a time of purging to prepare me for the purpose He had for my life. If I couldn't handle hard times, what kind of person would I be representing Him? I learned that the purging process was supposed to be a painful one. The Bible talked about God's children being refined like pure gold. I didn't understand what that meant until I learned that the process gold has to go through before its pure enough to sell is a long, ongoing one. The gold is melted down so the impurities can rise to the top and be skimmed off. That process is repeated until all the impurities are out. That's what God was doing through my circumstances. Each time He brought me through the fire, I was becoming a better, stronger person. I also learned that with all the religions in the world, Christianity is the only one that guarantees suffering. If the Savior of my soul had to suffer as much as He did, why did I expect to have it easy?

As I grew and took my faith seriously, others

around me saw the difference. I could say the same thing to the other girls that staff said to them and they listened to me. The staff started telling me they knew I was headed someplace – that my life wouldn't be wasted. I was going to be somebody.

During that time I was going to church on weekends with my boyfriend (the one who cheated on me) and I was learning things at that church I never knew. The pastor made Scripture come to life. It almost felt like he was talking straight to me as he preached every Sunday. He was teaching me how to apply God's word to my life and how to make it through the struggles, and how to fight the enemy so I could become the woman God wanted me to be.

He explained what it looked like to be a Christian in today's world without selling out and being a hypocrite. He painted word pictures of God's character that made me understand the One I served in a whole new way. The God I served and belonged to loved every part of me, knew me better than I knew myself, and stubbornly held onto me even as He disciplined me when I did things wrong.

As I learned to understand who God was, I learned what a real father is supposed to look like. It was foreign to me, yet it was exactly what I'd always wished my biological father was like. I learned that God is my protector, and that He uses the hard times in our lives for good things, even if we can't see it right away. I learned that my life experiences made me a stronger person, and that I would be able to use them to encourage other kids who were going through the same things. It was the first time someone had told me there was a purpose for the things I had been through – that they weren't just useless wastes in my life. God had plans for me that were bigger than I could take in at that time. All the heartache would have a point

I began to understand how wrong my thinking had been – believing what other people thought of me mattered. I started to see God's love for me as the most important thing in my life and all I really needed. I began wanting to be beautiful in His eyes, and learned from the pastor what a beautiful woman of God looks like: kind and compassionate to others, gentle, slow to anger, strong in character, not prideful . . . it was all so new to me.

The pastor talked about living a "God life"; a holy life because of a desire to please God, not to look good or get points. At that time, I stopped going to clubs and hanging around the wrong people. I was surprised to find out that I didn't miss them. God was so much more amazing that they looked pitiful and lost next to the joy and excitement of a relationship with Him.

The greatest lessons I learned were about letting go of the past. I was able to finally forgive all those who had hurt me. I didn't just say I was forgiving them – I actually did it. Once that happened, I could almost physically feel the mountains of emotional scars that defined me begin to heal.

I still had a lot of disappointments and set-backs, but I was growing. Mama was missing her appointments and since the goal was for us to reunite with her, each time she didn't do what she was supposed to, the whole process was put on hold. But, I didn't fall back into my despair. Now I had someone to lean on.

Finally Mama completed all her classes and requirements, and the court decided she was now responsible enough to take us back home with her. We were reunited in our childhood dream house and we had the hope that things would go much better than they had.

Mama tried so hard during those couple of months. She put us in counseling and joined us in family counseling. Unfortunately, she couldn't forgive herself. When we were young, she believed with her whole heart that she would always have a close relationship with us and that she was going to succeed in giving us the life she didn't have when she was a girl. She still had so much guilt because that hadn't happened, and depression had a strong hold on her.

She also hadn't had much interaction with us for the past ten to twelve months, so she had a hard time relating to her teenage daughters in the way she had when we were young. She condemned herself constantly and believed she deserved to be punished. She convinced herself that God was going to punish her over and over for her past mistakes. Daily, she remembered what things had been like when we were young and daily, she looked at the contrast between then and now. Things had fallen apart. She wouldn't let go of that or forgive herself.

After a couple months, Mama started spending time with the wrong people again, and falling into the same patterns and strongholds that had pulled her down before. We only had two options. Either we could go back to the children's homes or stay in the situation. I would have run away before going back to the children's home, so we didn't know what to do.

Thankfully, God was looking out for us, because a lady from our church, the pastor's sister, told us that God had put it on her heart to take all three of us into her home. She and her husband already had four sons, but she knew it was what they were supposed to do.

Mama went back to rehab or the psych ward for six months, and we stayed in the house with the lady we called Aunt Gloria. After awhile, Mama lost everything: her house, her car, and her dignity. During our phone conversations with her we could sometimes hear street noises and the sounds of cars going by. At those times, we knew she was either homeless, living on the street somewhere, or in a woman's shelter. Her only connection to us was through a payphone.

Toward the end of our sophomore year, we were sent back to live with Daddy. We had no idea what it would be like and we were a little scared. At that time, Regina and Daddy fought all the time and everyone knew the marriage was failing. Different women called the house all the time, he was still physically abusive to all of us, Regina was gambling more, and because there was no stability, my sisters and I forgot how awful it was being separated and started our fighting all over again.

Our first stretch of time living with Daddy was difficult, but he added a new dimension this time. He decided that at age sixteen, we were grown women and needed to be supporting ourselves instead of begging from him. We received monthly social security checks from Mama and each of us worked a part-time job, so Daddy decided that we should be paying rent and buying our own food. Many times he bought food for himself, but not for us, so our refrigerator was constantly empty. Sometimes Mama secretly left food for us on the doorstep or we stocked up or ate too much when we got the opportunity for food, because we didn't know how long it would be before our next meal. We were afraid to say anything to Daddy, so we did what we could to survive on our own.

By this time, my sisters were going to church with me and had a personal relationship with Jesus Christ like I did. One day Ayisha went and got her camera, opened the refrigerator door, and took a picture of the empty shelves. She said, "Years from now, when we're successful and have overflowing cupboards, we're going to look at this picture and remember where the Lord brought us from. God will give us enough food that we'll never go hungry again."

Finally during our junior year, Daddy beat Regina up so badly that she pressed charges and he was forced to leave the house. He went to stay with his brother for almost a year while the divorce was being processed and we stayed with Regina. That was a turning point in our relationship with her.

After he was gone, all four of us became a support system for each other. There was a lot more peace in the house and we settled into a routine that worked for us. We had always known that when he was home, she treated us differently than when he was away, but it was the first time that we were able to really get to know her for herself. We didn't see Daddy much during that year and we were okay.

During this time, my sisters and I got much closer to the pastor of our church, Bishop Jones, and his family. We considered him and his wife the father and mother we should have had, but never did. He took care of us in ways that made us cry in gratitude, because they were so much more than we could have dreamed.

One Sunday, he began describing some girls to

the congregation that needed a lot of love and support. He gave them a little background on what these girls had been through and what the church's responsibility was in taking care of them. I sat still, listening to him, not realizing what he was about to do. After his description of these girls, he called my sisters and I forward. He explained to them that we had very little, and anyone who was led needed to come up and put money at our feet, partly because we were orphans in a sense, but also to show us we were not alone. All we could do was stand there and cry as streams of people came and put money at our feet. It was one of the most humbling, beautiful moments of my life, and I felt God's love surrounding me through His people in a way I didn't realize was possible.

Toward the end of our senior year, Bishop Jones, who we referred to as "Dad" because that's what he had become to us, found out that we didn't have anything to go to our senior prom with, and he didn't think it was right for us to miss a special occasion like that because of our circumstances. He gave each of us a generous amount of money to go shopping for our dresses, pay for anything else we wanted for the evening, and even some extra for our own use.

By the time prom came around, I felt like a princess. It was my night and I felt truly beautiful. I looked back on where I had come from, hardly knowing when my next meal would be, wondering where my mother was, fearing another beating by my father, and I knew with everything in me that God had kept me alive from the time I was a tiny baby for this moment and the times that were ahead of me. Everyday, He was showing me how much He loved me and that all those times I had felt like life was hopeless, He was with me, giving me strength to take another breath, another step.

When it was close to time for my sisters and I to graduate, Bishop told us he was going to take me and my sisters to college. Bishop and his wife already had three daughters to pay for, but they looked at us as their own daughters and wanted to do this for us.

Ayisha and I went to a school in Tennessee and while we were there, God put it on our hearts to start a Christian sorority. The goal was for young Christian women to come together, have account-ability, and strive together toward holiness. We learned a lot about starting a business and the requirements included in maintaining something of that size, but we decided that if the secular world could do it, how much more we should be able to. We needed to provide a place for all young women, despite their social status, to come together and grow in their relationship with Jesus Christ with others who had the same desire.

During this time, Ayisha and I knew Mama wasn't doing well, so we moved her down with us. She went through a lot of struggles and we tried to get her into a rehab program, but things weren't working like we had hoped.

During my first year in college, I had a couple casual boyfriends, but I became friends with a young man named Bruce. I talked to him a lot, but I told my friends and Ayisha that I thought he was kind of strange. I wasn't interested in him at all but, after awhile, I started falling in love with his character and spirit. He loved the Lord and was growing as a man of God faster than I was growing in my own walk, even though he became a Christian later than I did. My best friend, one of Bishop's daughters, told me that Bruce and I would end up together, and I told her she was crazy. What I didn't know was that she saw something more than what I saw. She could see how our personalities complimented each other, how he would lead a home with strength and humility, and how much he would cherish me. It took God getting the little boys out of my life to open my eyes to the man Bruce was.

We began dating during college and he was my best friend. We both had such busy lives that we weren't one of those couples that are always together and exclude others. We made sure we spent time with each other, but we didn't stop our other activities. During my junior year, Bruce proposed to me and of course, I said yes. I still knew he was silly, but I knew him as a man of strong character, and I had no doubt that he was God's man for me.

During this time, things were not going well with Mama. She was sick with cancer and believed it would be better for her to come back to her hometown. I just didn't know how sick she was. I eventually moved back home to take care of her. During that time, she led me to believe she was now cancer free. However, the truth was that her doctor had only given her six months to a year to live. This became a living nightmare for me. Thoughts of losing her made me sick to my stomach. I returned back to my hometown in a hurry to move in with my mom. She started making positive changes in her life and I could see the change all over her.

I knew I needed to work, so I prayed that God would open doors for me to get full-time employment. I was driving past the children's home where I had stayed for ten months and saw a sign that they were hiring. I knew what those kids were going through and that I could help them in a way others hadn't been able to help me while I was there. I had been in their shoes. I was also living proof of what can happen to a broken heart and life when Jesus Christ takes over.

It didn't take long for me to go through the application process and some of the people I knew from my time as a resident were still working there, but in different positions. They loved the idea of a former resident working there, maybe because it made them feel like their work was a success and that there were some residents who turned out alright.

I started as a house parent, working a full week on and then having a full week off. Unfortunately, my body couldn't handle the stress of those long hours, so I became sick often. I built a relationship with the residents quickly and knew my time with them needed to be longer, so I changed to a shift position. I had a bond with the residents that was unique and strong, because I had been one of them. They knew I understood, but that also gave me permission to challenge them to become more than what the world told them they could be. I taught them truths from Scripture constantly, and openly talked about what God was doing in my life and what He wanted to do with them.

God blessed me with a great group of co-workers and we were all on fire for Christ, but also had a passion for the kids. We worked as one when it came to loving them and disciplining them. We created a safe environment where they felt like people actually cared for them. As I worked with them and my co-workers and friends came alongside me, the girls matured and grew, asking questions about God and who Jesus is, admitting anger and feelings of betrayal that He had allowed painful things to happen to them, and confusion of not knowing what to do. I remembered my own struggles and was able to meet them where they were. I became a mother figure for them and protected them with everything in me, while teaching them to be the best they could be. I didn't let them believe they had an excuse to fail just because of where they had come from. I was proof that they could succeed.

During my time at the children's home, major life-changing events happened. Some were cause for rejoicing, but others were painful seasons that God alone carried me through.

I married my best friend in the chapel on the grounds of the children's home, but the preparations were difficult. God brought many people into my life who volunteered services as wedding gifts, such as the catering and flowers. I didn't have much money and I was terrified about asking Daddy for any, because I knew he would cuss me out and tell me how greedy I was being, using him for things like that. But I finally asked. Yes, he did what I expected, but then on my wedding day, he walked me down the aisle. I asked Bishop to do it, but he said, "Aileen, that place is rightfully your father's. If he won't do it, then I would be honored, but you need to ask him first." I was hurt by that, but I understood it was the right thing to do, even if it felt fake to me. No one watching us walk toward my groom could see into my story or into the past of all that had happened between Daddy and me, but I knew.

Chapter Ten

The Story of Tanya

Forgiveness = Freedom

Tanya

Chapter 10 – Forgiveness = Freedom

"For if you forgive men their trespasses, your heavenly Father will also forgive you"

(Matthew 6:14).

When Tanya was eleven years old, she was placed in a children's home. She was terrified. Her mama went from being a successful single mama with a career, to a drug addict living from relationship to relationship and drug fix to drug fix. She wasn't taking care of Tanya and her brother like she was supposed to, and the state took them away.

Most of the other kids at the children's home were older than Tanya and a lot tougher. She was so scared. She put on a grown-up attitude and tried to make her own place there, but it was only a mask. After a month, she moved to the longer term residential cottage and met a group of staff who loved her and helped her realize she could still be a little girl – she didn't have to be afraid.

A year later, she was released to go live with a relative. Within weeks she found out she had bone cancer. Through this horrible experience her mother was faced with a possibility she had never thought of – losing a child. It made her see her life for what it was and she broke down. She cried out to God for help and knew that she couldn't do things the old way anymore. She had to do something drastic. She gave her life to Jesus Christ and became a new woman. She put herself into a drug rehab center, got a job, and did everything she could to make herself worthy of getting her kids back.

Tanya's mama was faithfully by her side through all the chemotherapy treatments and struggles that go along with cancer. As her mother became the woman she was supposed to be, Tanya began to see hope. They both realized that through terrible circumstances, God lovingly came by their sides and turned bad situations into good. For the first time, they understood that they didn't have to walk through life alone. The one who created them wanted to be there with them, guiding them, helping them, and loving them through everything.

Today Tanya, her brother and their mama are walking with Jesus Christ as a family. They still have some hard days, but they are together and looking to God. He was the only one who could turn their lives from mess into joy, and He is the one who helps them now.

Chapter 10 – Forgiveness = Freedom

My wedding was a celebration. It was both beautiful and alive. I cried out of gratitude that God had pulled me out of the pit I was in and brought me into this. I was marrying a man who loved me dearly, but loved God above me and desired to help me grow into the woman my heavenly Father made me to be. I was surrounded by friends and family who held me up and supported me when I could hardly put one foot in front of the other. My godfather (Bishop Jones) performed the ceremony and covered us with blessings for our new life together. It couldn't have gone more perfectly. And I looked beautiful. I felt beautiful and I couldn't believe it was really me in that place. Bruce and I wrote vows to each other that were so personal, but it seemed right for our friends and family to hear those words that were meant only for each other.

I had gotten special permission from work for my girls to attend the wedding. It was important to me that they see what a godly relationship was like and the beautiful, sacred thing God had meant marriage to be. Our honeymoon to Jamaica was our time to become one and fall even more in love with each other than we already were. When I went back to work with the girls, I was a newlywed who had been blessed beyond words.

What I had learned long before was that life never stays all good or all bad. Things were going so well, it made sense that a huge trial was about to come. Bishop always said that for every successful story, there is often a painful road that leads the way to success. In the Christian life, there are mountain-top experiences when it seems like God is so close and everything is great, but there are also valleys when God alone can help us through. It was about time for some valleys.

I had been praying for both of my parents – that God would protect them, but more importantly, show them how much they needed Him. I finally told my mother how I felt. I wanted her to know how much I loved her, but that it was tearing me up to see her destroying her life. It finally got through to her. She could see, by God's grace, what it was doing to us, her girls who loved her so much, to see her running away from being the woman we knew she could be. She began attending church faithfully and said to me, "Aileen, I finally saw what my actions were doing to you. I want to change. I don't want to put you and your sisters through this anymore." I have to admit that she had disappointed me so many times before that I wasn't sure if she would follow through, but God is bigger than any of our problems and I knew if anyone could change her from the inside out, it was Him.

I wanted them to realize how broken they were and how much they needed a Savior. God heard my prayers, but His answer was not what I expected. The worse day of my life was when I received a phone call from my sister saying my mother, who was sick and suffering for a long time, was not breathing. After hearing the fear and depression in her voice, I immediately went to check on her. By the time I arrived at my mother's house, it was too late. The paramedics said that she had been gone for too long and there was nothing they could do to save her. My heart dropped and everything I knew came to a stop. My sister and I came together and cried, feeling so helpless, yet urgently desiring to go see her one more time. How could it all be over so soon? I had so many plans for us. For several days I cried and begged God for mercy, wishing I could change the hand of time. I became so depressed, needing some type of answers. Why did she have to leave so soon, why did my heart hurt so badly . . . why, why, why?

During this time I tried to cling to my father. Daddy tried his best to uplift me as much as possible. This was one of the first times that I felt his love for me. After several days of being completely helpless to do anything other than pray and cry my heart out to God, I received a answer from God. I could hear him saying, **"For My thoughts are not your thoughts, Nor are your ways My ways," says the Lord (Isaiah 55:8).** I never knew so many emotions could happen at one time. I went from sobbing until I couldn't cry anymore, to numbness, to denial, to pleading with God to explain to me why He let my mother die when I was praying for a miracle, to more crying, to feeling like I was out of control. Through it all, my loved ones held onto me and cried with me, and God gave me comfort, but also the freedom to be honest with Him, even if it meant crying out to Him in confusion, pain, and sometimes even anger. Even the smallest decisions were overwhelming. I felt like I was walking in slow motion through a dream that I couldn't wake up from. Now I can truly say, "Who Said I Wouldn't Make It."

As I talked with Daddy, I told him that I would pray for him and he thanked me, which is more than he would have done before. Even through the pain, I knew God was working on him, but that the hardest hearts sometimes take longer to reach. Sometimes it also takes something that extreme to get the person's attention.

While all this was happening, I was running into some problems at work. Most of my friends and co-workers had resigned and were replaced by staff who did not understand my girls or my methods of working with them. I had little respect left for my supervisor because of lies he had told, and his attempts to ruin my character with slander. I finally came to the point when I knew I would not be able to be effective with my girls anymore in that setting, and that the best option was to look for another position and become a visiting resource for them on weekends. Within days I was hired for a nanny position and knew God was releasing me from the children's home. Yet, in His goodness, He allowed me to remain part of their lives, seeing them regularly and teaching them even more about Him.

During all this, God had put it on my heart to talk with my co-workers who had resigned about starting a transitional living program for at-risk girls. They all had the same heart for kids that I do, and I had believed ever since I was a resident in the children's home that I wanted to start my own one day. After my negative experiences as a worker and a resident, I knew I needed to follow through with my dreams and create a home that would be more suited to the needs of hurting youth. They needed a place where they felt valued and were taught values that would help them succeed in life. They needed to see Christlike behavior from the adults in their world, and the chance to be discipled by women who really loved the Lord and loved them. As I began working with this group of women, I began to see God work. We started from scratch and as we continued working and praying, God brought people into our lives who helped guide us and teach us what we needed to get this program started and make it succeed.

Through the years, God has brought healing to my family in so many ways. Daddy calls sometimes now to ask how things are going or to find out how a special speaking engagement went. When we tell him we'll pray for him, instead of cursing at us, he says, "You do that," which is my father's way is saying he's more open to that. I've learned to let my mother's death be a stepping stone to victory. Our stepmom, Regina, became almost like a real mother to me as I grew into a woman, and she came to know the Lord personally. Many times I have gone over to her house to rejoice with her over good news or to lay my head on her lap and cry as I suffer through a trial. She has been there for my sisters and I faithfully, and continues to support us as young women and as sisters in Christ. This may not be your happy ending, but to me it's more than what I ever imagined God doing for me. I am convinced that the best is yet to come. Finally, I learned that pain produces change. Every test, trail, and storm in your life is designed to make you a stronger and wiser person. So, hold on and never give up on the promises of God. I made it! I finally have peace.

"Finally, be strong in the Lord and in <u>His</u> mighty power. Put on the full armor of God so that you can take your stand against the devil's schemes. For our struggle is not against flesh and blood, but against the rulers, against the authorities, against the powers of this dark world and against the spiritual forces of evil in the heavenly realms. Therefore, put on the full armor of God, so that when the day of evil comes, you may be able to stand your ground, and after you have done everything, to stand" (Ephesians 6:10-13).

"The Lord your God is with you, He is mighty to save. He will take great delight in you, He will quiet you with His love, He will rejoice over you with singing" (Zephaniah 3:17).

"He who dwells in the shelter of the Most High will rest in the shadow of the Almighty. I will say of the Lord, 'He is my refuge and my fortress, my God, in whom I trust'" (Psalm 91:1-2).

CPSIA information can be obtained
at www.ICGtesting.com
Printed in the USA
BVOW08s2312271116
468956BV00001B/2/P